DIGITAL MARKETING MBA

DIGITAL MARKETING MBA

Guiding Principles for Researching, Planning, and Managing a Marketing Strategy to Transform Your Business

David J. Bradley, MBA

Copyright © 2019 by David J. Bradley. All rights reserved. Except as permitted under section 107 or 108 of the U.S. Copyright Act of 1976, no part of this publication may be reproduced, distributed, or transmitted in any form or by any means or stored in a database or retrieval system, without the prior written permission of the publisher. Permission should be requested in written form and sent to Bbg, Inc., 536 Atwells Ave., 2nd Floor, Providence, RI 02909.

This document is geared towards providing exact and reliable information regarding the topic and issue covered. The publication is sold with the idea that the publisher is not required to render, officially permitted, or otherwise, qualified services. If advice is necessary, legal or professional, a practiced individual in the profession should be ordered. From a Declaration of Principles which was accepted and approved equally by a Committee of the American Bar Association and a Committee of Publishers and Associations.

The information provided herein is stated to be truthful and consistent, in that any liability, in terms of inattention or otherwise, by any usage or abuse of any policies, processes, or directions contained within is the solitary and utter responsibility of the recipient reader. Under no circumstances will any legal responsibility or blame be held against the publisher for any reparation, damages, or monetary loss due to the information herein, either directly or indirectly.

Respective authors own all copyrights not held by the publisher. The information herein is offered for informational purposes solely. The presentation of the information is without contract or any type of guarantee assurance. Trademarks used are without any consent, and the publication of the trademark is without permission or backing by the trademark owner. All trademarks and brands within this book are for clarifying purposes only, unaffiliated, and are the owned by the owners themselves.

This book is dedicated to the readers and students who trusted me to educate them about digital marketing through Getting Digital Marketing Right, *published in 2015, exceeding a reach of ten thousand. Your support and feedback fueled me to create this book. Thank you.*

CONTENTS

PREFACE ix
   How This Book Was Designed x
      A-E-E: Adherence, Effectiveness, and Efficiency x
      D^3 Principle: Dissecting, Discriminating, Distributing xi
   Online Resources xiii

INTRODUCTION 1
   Roadblock One: What Do We Know? 2
   Roadblock Two: What Do We Do? 2
   Roadblock Three: How Do We Execute? 3
   Begin with the RACI Chart 4

PHASE 1: MARKET INTELLIGENCE 7
   1.1 Mine Intelligence Assets 9
      1.1.1 Market Research 10
      1.1.2 Databases & Lists 12
      1.1.3 Buyer Personas 14
      1.1.4 Sales Processes 15
      1.1.5 Sales Scripts & Standards 17
      1.1.6 Sales & Marketing Collateral 18
      1.1.7 Customer Experience Maps 19
   1.2 Gather Intelligence Data 20
      1.2.1 Marketing Questionnaire 20
      1.2.2 Marketing & Technology Inventory 22
      1.2.3 Program Gap Assessment 25
      1.2.4 Competitive Intel 26
      1.2.5 Interviewing Key Stakeholders 35
      1.2.6 Focus Groups 39
      1.2.7 Mass Surveying 40
      1.2.8 Buyer Persona Development 41
   Phase 1 Conclusion 44

PHASE 2: STRATEGY DEVELOPMENT.......................... 47
  2.1 Review Processes & Technology 49
    2.1.1 Online Value Proposition........................ 49
    2.1.2 Digital Touchpoints 51
    2.1.3 Digital Marketing Funnels 53
    2.1.4 Customer Experience Innovations................ 56
    2.1.5 Customer Loyalty Programming.................. 58
    2.1.6 Marketing Technology (MarTech) 60
    2.1.7 Evaluating Your Website As Your Central Hub 69
  2.2 Select Communication Channels..................... 72
    2.2.1 Pull: Content Marketing 73
    2.2.2 Push: Paid Advertising 85
  Phase 2 Conclusion...................................... 95

PHASE 3: GUIDED IMPLEMENTATION 97
  3.1 Identify the Execution Team 99
    3.1.1 Agile Marketing Methodology.................... 99
    3.1.2 In-House & Outsourcing....................... 104
    3.1.3 Restructuring Your Marketing Department....... 107
    3.1.4 Budget Reallocation........................... 109
  3.2 Establish Management Protocols 111
    3.2.1 Measurement, KPI Tracking & Campaign
        Optimizations 111
    3.2.2 Ongoing Employee & Executive Training......... 118
    3.2.3 Quarterly Strategy Reviews 120
    3.2.4 SOPs & Systemization 121
  Phase 3 Conclusion..................................... 123

FINAL THOUGHTS 125

  Online Resources 127
  About the Author....................................... 128

PREFACE

This book is all about developing a digital strategy. It's helpful to know the strategic process before you begin planning so that you know what comes next and how different pieces will fit together and help you in the future.

I recommend that you read through this book taking highlights and notes as you go, then return to the "Guiding Principles" as you begin to execute. First, learn the process and philosophies, and then apply them.

You don't have to follow this recommendation, but I do believe it will be more effective and shouldn't slow you down. In fact, I think it will empower you, maintaining momentum by understanding the full process and vision of what you are creating.

Furthermore, you will see a "Guiding Principle" in each section. You can review this short, 2-3 sentence overview for each section. These serve to help you understand how to better process the material and develop your own concrete mental frameworks. They will jog your memory should you forget the purpose behind that section, too.

Remember to download the bonuses, as well, noted near the end of this book. You can find these at **DavidJBradley.com/digital-mba-resources**/. These will make your life a bit easier as you engage in the activities.

This book came to fruition from my noticing a common a lack of managerial or executive-level education in the market on this topic. I have found no book that provides a philosophical and practical approach to addressing digital, free of the hype and focus on the "internet marketing guru" audience. I wanted a resource that the average business owner or leader would be able to understand, appreciate, and use.

The approach that I share with you has been derived from my personal experiences. You will find proven theories that I have developed, practiced, and implemented across clients and across industries. I have learned from dozens of sources, including major publications, as well as individuals I've worked with.

I implore you to make a concerted effort in developing a comprehensive digital plan and modern marketing mind. Many see digital marketing as an expense. Because it is. Because there is no thoughtful approach to creating a comprehensive strategy behind digital. Because there are mixed messages about digital and a lack of sophistication and experience in the area. My plan is to change that for you in the pages ahead.

How This Book Was Designed

This book was written with two design frameworks in mind. I share them below as they are mental models that may help you in your career.

This is not the start of your marketing learning, though they are philosophies you can apply to marketing. Feel free to skip to the next chapter if you would rather jump into things now.

A-E-E: Adherence, Effectiveness, and Efficiency

Adherence means "will the reader actually read and apply the learnings from the book." Effectiveness means "will these actions provide the reader with the desired result."

Efficiency means "will the goal be achieved in a timely manner."

To be sure these three objectives are met, we first need to define what the goal is. My goal with this book is to provide a set of principles, philosophies, and frameworks that are proven and timeless. If you return to this book in five years, the core tenets should still hold true. I'm not here to teach you about what's hot in marketing today; I'm here to share *ways of thinking* that you can carry forth throughout your career.

The intended outcome of this is the ability to converse with digital marketers of various sorts, identify meaningful strategies, and follow best practices. Whether you are developing a digital plan from the ground up or iterating on what exists in your company today, you should feel confident that you are working with quality data, that you are capable of evaluating any digital expert's opinions, and that you can make decisions that are intelligent for your business.

My commitment to you is that if you *adhere* to the process, the process will be *effective* and you will find *efficiency* through quick application of the learnings.

D^3 *Principle: Dissecting, Discriminating, Distributing*

I looked at the vast amount of information currently available on "digital marketing," and I took on the perspective of an executive seeking to understand what they need to do in their leadership role, and nothing more, in order to make intelligent decisions about digital. This was part of a D^3 principle: *Dissecting, Discriminating, Distributing*.

In *Dissecting*, I separated the components of digital and ancillary topics into separate areas, so each was as narrowly defined and isolated as possible. In *Discriminating*, I analyzed each isolated area and determined what is most relevant to an executive and which are less relevant. I then began making notes on key highlights of the individual area that would be most relevant. This part of the process relies heavily on the 80/20 rule: what 20% needs to be examined that would provide 80% of the knowledge needed.

In *Distributing*, I created a framework for these key areas in an order that will allow you to best understand them and their interconnectedness. This allows you to begin applying the knowledge right away, without requiring information found in later chapters.

It is important to me that this isn't simply another book on marketing, but that it serves as a timeless resource you can rely on as you continue developing your strategic marketing mind. I hope the philosophies and principles you find in the pages ahead will serve as a guiding light.

Online Resources

We are going to cover a wide variety of material in the pages ahead. One of the most important aspects of success is being organized and efficient. Unfortunately, organization itself is typically inefficient upfront due to the time and intellectual energy that goes into creation of templates, systems, and processes.

That's why I created an online repository of all resources you will need in this process. You can find this at **DavidJBradley.com/digital-mba-resources/**. In this repository, you will find resources including:

- Questionnaires and information gathering tools
- Charts, templates, and tools
- Spreadsheets and assessments
- Buyer persona templates
- Stakeholder interview guides

You will also find my email address to reach me directly with the one word to use in the subject line to be sure your email will be read. Questions are appreciated. They help me revise my books and presentations.

Best,
David J. Bradley, MBA

INTRODUCTION

Four years ago, I published *Getting Digital Marketing Right*, a five-step digital strategy process I developed through mixing disciplines and experiences into one cohesive plan.

I'm proud of that book. It was my first real foray into writing, and it has and continues to serve a meaningful purpose. It became a bestseller for a while, sold very well ... and the sales continue today!

Of course, my own thinking has evolved and changed since then. A lot happens in three years, and I believe my process has become more sophisticated and comprehensive. And now, this is my attempt to make it simple. Simple enough for anyone to pick up this book and create a truly comprehensive strategy for their organization.

Nonetheless, my first book is still an excellent choice for marketers and small business owners. This book, however, provides a deeper sophistication to the strategy process, appropriate for veteran marketers, executives, and leaders alike.

I have found three common roadblocks that almost every company faces – from startup to enterprise – when looking to further their investment and integration in digital.

Roadblock One: What Do We Know?

Whether you are a marketer, business owner, or otherwise, be honest... Marketers operate on an assumption basis far more often than is healthy! Thinking one knows the market compared to diving into the data that proves your assumptions are two very different things.

I challenge you to approach this plan as a scientist, rather than as another marketer. Don't make it up as you go. Discover and understand both quantitative and qualitative data.

Roadblock Two: What Do We Do?

If you didn't address the first roadblock, you will certainly face this one. To know what you need to do in order to market your business digitally, you need to have real data to support your plan.

We know there are endless options to reach your market online, and most can work if you have a strong enough campaign strategy. But among the many options, I am sure it's important to you that you choose the most efficient and effective channels, right?

Prioritize intelligently and strategically.

Roadblock Three: How Do We Execute?

Implementing and executing a plan is where many struggle, regardless of the financial resources the company has available.

How you actually *execute* the plan that you designed, and *continue to do so successfully*, is a challenge. Part of the problem is getting the right teams in place in a way that makes sense, and part of the problem is a management issue.

Things fall apart because of one of three reasons:

1. nothing happens,
2. no leadership is provided, or
3. teams in place do not have the knowledge, skills and abilities to be successful.

These three roadblocks are where most of us stumble, simply due to a lack of information, a lack of planning, and a lack of execution capabilities.

Digital creates market leaders through better ways to capture the attention of customers and to interact with them according to new nuances of our culture.

What you are about to read, in my opinion, is the first book that provides a proven process to help create a reliable digital strategy. This is not how to build a campaign, but a complete communications plan.

My goal was to apply two principles in writing this book: brevity and efficacy.

So, why don't I stop now and let you dive in?

Begin with the RACI Chart

Any time I begin a project involving multiple parties, I document roles and responsibilities according to a RACI chart, also known as a *RACI matrix* or *responsibilities assignment matrix* or a *linear responsibility chart*.

The chart is helpful because it provides formal documentation of *who is supposed to do what*. This may sound simple, yet countless times when working in teams, we experience otherwise. Miscommunications, waning enthusiasm, or blatant neglect of responsibility is a real occurrence.

Aside from avoiding negatives, I find that this creates more balance, clearer expectations, and fairer distribution among teams. It is important to start a project with vigor and to execute the project with clarity. The RACI chart appears as follows:

	Element 1	Element 2	Element 3
Responsible			
Accountable			
Consult			
Inform			

The chart should have three to five Strategic Elements. Less, and you may be too general in the areas of focus. More, and you are likely to find it overwhelming. Align the elements to your situation and project.

It is important that all parties involved are clear on what each role means: Responsible, Accountable, Consult, and Inform.

Responsible parties are those who perform the work within that element. *Accountable* parties are those who provide approvals and make final decisions. *Consulting* parties are those who others go to when seeking guidance, feedback, or contribution. *Informed* parties are those who must be kept apprised of projects, tasks, and outcomes relative to that element.

In considering who is relevant, make sure that you include internal *and external* parties. This includes agencies, consultants, internal domain experts, project managers, and leadership teams.

This is a concept that transfers across domains, so do not limit yourself to using RACI with marketing alone. In any project you undertake, you can incorporate this as part of your strategic process.

To get you started, here is an example of how you may develop a RACI chart for your digital strategy development. This will make more sense as you explore the book.

	Market Intelligence	**Digital Processes & Technology**	**Communication Channels**	**Guided Implementation**
Responsible	Dave from Marketing	MarTech Consultant, Marketing Team	Consultants, Agency Partners	Marketing Team, Agency Partners, Consultants
Accountable	CMO	CTO & CMO	CMO	CMO
Consult	Sales Team, Customer Service Team	Technology Team	Marketing Team	Leadership Team
Inform	Leadership Team, Marketing Team	Leadership Team, Sales Team	Leadership Team, Customer Service Team	Leadership Team

Note, however, that there can be additional charts created for sub-projects within.

PHASE I
MARKET INTELLIGENCE

The Market Intelligence phase is where we collect new and existing information about our market, consumers, business operations, as well as any associated helpful information.

This phase is split into two core components: mining intelligence assets and gathering intelligence data. I can tell you with certainty that data is the cornerstone of successful marketing and strategy. So, that becomes our starting point.

I understand it can be exciting to jump straight into creating a marketing campaign with creative concepts and potential for "quick wins." However, both short and long-term benefits will expand in business impact when you step back and thoughtfully consider what you are trying to accomplish and what information can help you do that.

This phase is incredibly important because it provides a competitive edge to your company that others cannot replicate without their own market intelligence process. The competitive edge that this information provides allows you to outthink competitors, rather than attempt to outspend them. As you can imagine, the benefits of this become exponential.

> **Guiding Principle:** Your Market Intelligence process, and the data derived from it, provides a competitive edge. Do not underestimate its power and resourcefulness.

1.1
MINE INTELLIGENCE ASSETS

Let us first define "Intelligence Assets." Intelligence Assets are elements that exist in your business today and are readily or easily available for you to examine, interpret, and turn into actionable insights.

To clarify further, examples of "elements" include past market research, databases and lists, customer reviews, past campaign creative, and historical performance reports. You can use this existing data and information to shortcut the research process, saving time and money.

This will allow you to effectively and appropriately allocate resources to research and new discoveries while avoiding double-work.

These assets may expose strengths and weaknesses to your message, they may reveal your customers' most compelling hot buttons, and they may uncover opportunities that were previously overlooked or not capitalized on.

The concept is simple: if we don't have to reinvent the wheel, let's not. Let's stay agile. Let's take advantage of quick and easy wins.

> **Guiding Principle:** Intelligence Assets already exist in your business and can easily be located and leveraged to your advantage. Tap into these elements and interpret the insights they provide on your business, market, competitors, successes, and failures.

1.1.1
Market Research

Previously conducted market research can be helpful today. However, always apply a healthy skepticism when considering *how* this research was collected, *when* it was collected, and *if* it is still relevant.

As a rule of thumb, research conducted within the last five years is more probable to still have validity, if it was conducted in a scientific manner. If the research is over five years old, be wary of its utility. With the speed and frequency of change in the modern consumers' behavior and the digital landscape, older information may be more harmful than helpful.

Depending on a number of factors – your role, your tenure, your company size, changes in ownership – you may or may not know instantly whether market research was previously conducted by your company or a third-party firm. If uncertain, please take a moment to write an email to others who may be aware if there had been research conducted previously.

Let's take a moment to discuss *how* to get this information from others because within the explanation will be important marketing strategies for today's consumer.

Now, in case you are in a circumstance where you know getting your hands on the report will take diligent follow-up with another party who "owns" it, such as the head of marketing, here's how you want to begin:

Hi Tom,

A one-word reply from you will help me quite a bit! As I think about our digital strategy, collecting any and all existing information will be helpful to us.

I was wondering if we had market research conducted for our company within the past five years? Simply answering "yes" or "no" will let me know if this is something I should investigate further or take off my to-do list at this time.

Thank you.

Feel free to tailor to your personal style, but the main premise of how we are positioning our request is to make it as easy as possible for this other party to let you know whether the information exists. We don't want the email to go unanswered, or to receive a "no" when it should be a "yes" because answering in the affirmative would require additional work on their part.

Everyone always feels busy in their own life, so don't add more work to their plate, particularly if not appropriate for *you* to do so. If you are the superior in this situation, you may be more direct. Again, this example is written for *compliance*, rather than depth. That comes in your follow-up.

Nonetheless, I share this because it speaks to how you want your marketing to be consumed: with ease. That comes from a customer-first approach.

Don't stop at your company's market research. Look for third-party sources who have conducted research on your industry, as well. Seek out industry associations for their provided resources and make a phone call to learn more about what they can provide. Even if they don't have publicly accessible reports, they may enlighten you on how to access more industry information.

You may also consider sources such as IBISWorld, who offer industry research reports, or Think with Google, including their Zero Moment of Truth (ZMOT) studies. There are plenty of major consultancies, advisories, and publications that provide industry insights and reports.

You can also use a little savvy Google searching to your advantage. From the search engine, lead your search query for an industry report with "filetype:pdf." This will present PDF documents exclusively in the search results, which is the file format that actual reports are typically created within.

For example, to learn about how the Millennial market thinks and acts about mortgages, search for "filetype:pdf mortgages for Millennials research report." This may help to identify actual reports and should take you five minutes of searching time.

> **Guiding Principle:** Be optimistic yet skeptical about existing market research. If conducted well and still relevant to today's world, you may gain great insights. This is not limited to your own research, so also prioritize finding research conducted on your industry or market by third-parties.

1.1.2
Databases & Lists

Database marketing is as powerful as ever. In recent years, multi-channel touchpoints have become more popular.

This is inclusive of direct mail, email, SMS/text messaging, and voicemail drops.

But before we can consider *how* to reach out to the lists we have, we need to know *what* lists we have. Then, we need to confirm and improve quality of these lists.

There are several lists you want to collect: prospective customers, current customers, past customers, and lost prospects. How you define "customers" and if other lists are relevant will be to your discretion. Perhaps lists of strategic partners or vendors are helpful? Make note of that.

I recommend you keep track of these lists in a spreadsheet. In this spreadsheet, keep note of the list file name, list purpose, list size, how contacts are added to that list, the last time the list has been cleansed, and what other lists may have related data. Any additional notes that someone should know about the list can be added here, as well.

Once the lists have been collected, let's look to "clean" them. This is the act of removing contacts who are not likely to be relevant to your marketing going forward. For example, if you have a prospective customer list that you email monthly and someone has not opened the last four emails you sent out, you may wish to remove him/her from the list. Likewise, when you have a bad email address or your emails bounce with a certain contact, you may wish to remove them, as well.

Consider this cleansing activity as a way to ensure your reputation as a contact is high. The higher percentage of people who open emails, the higher your deliverability of emails to inboxes (and not spam folders) is, the stronger your reputation becomes and the stronger your marketing can be. Besides, we want strong lists, not long lists.

Cleaning also has to do with making sure your records are organized and clear. Here are steps to follow in your list cleansing process:

1. Merge duplicate contacts.
2. Consider removal of inactive contacts who have gone dormant for a significant amount of time.
3. Make sure remaining records use consistent syntaxes for their information (such as "CA" versus "California" to denote state).
4. Finally, remove any remaining contacts that are clearly fake based on the email address or phone number (e.g., 555-555-5555, xyz@domain.com).

A clean database improves deliverability, reduces waste, and is a simple, good tactic of proper marketing. After doing this, update the spreadsheet with a new column listing the post-cleaning list size. This may indicate the overall list quality, depending on the extent of list size change.

> **Guiding Principle:** Lists can be tremendously powerful to you. However, we always want to make sure we have high quality lists, rather than high volume lists. This is measured based upon data accuracy and list member engagement.

1.1.3
Buyer Personas

Buyer personas are fictional representations of your *best* customers. The persona is based on real data collected about customer demographics and online behavior, as well as with educated assumption of personal histories, motivations, and concerns.

Note: One of my major gripes with marketers is that we use too many terms for the same thing! "Avatars," "ideal customer profiles," "buyer personas"...they're all the same thing.

The way that we know who our customers are, what they're thinking, and how they behave online is by defining buyer personas. This can be an involved process, but remember, at this stage, we are simply looking for *existing* data. So, check with marketing, sales, and customer service teams to see if personas exist in your company today.

(If you are still unsure of what this looks like, you can skip to the *Buyer Persona Development* segment in the "Gathering Intelligence Data" section of this book.)

> **Guiding Principle:** Communications live and die by having accurate, up-to-date and comprehensive buyer personas to serve as guides. They help develop consistent, clear, and relevant communications with and understandings of your customer for everyone in your company. This is particularly important for marketing, sales, and customer service teams.

1.1.4
Sales Processes

What do you know about how relationships are handled today – from first contact, to point of sale, and after someone becomes a customer? If you do not have each step of this process mapped out already, you should do that now.

You can handle this with pen and paper or in a presentation document. Each step and how it is connected to other steps throughout the process must be simple and clear. Connections, or lack thereof, are important to visualize.

Start at the beginning by identifying how people may contact your company first. For example, inquiring on the website, them calling in, or your sales team cold calling them.

What's the next step? We are not looking at what is said or asked, but the next stage of the sales process. If you have multiple options again, list those out. We are not here now to analyze what "should" happen or what needs to be changed or improved. We simply want to know what is currently happening.

Continue until the point of sale when someone becomes a customer. Only stop at this point if contact stops there. If there are elements such as ongoing communication with current or past customers, requests for referrals, or upsells, this should be documented in the sales process, too.

> **Guiding Principle:** Knowing the sales process today will help us identify where digital can integrate in the future, as well as general improvement to the sales processes at a future time. You can't optimize, systemize, or train for what is not well documented.

1.1.5
Sales Scripts & Standards

With the sales process defined, seek out any and all scripts and standards found throughout the sales process. Standards may be generally accepted or officially documented practices that salespeople use when communicating or negotiating with prospects.

For example, some companies have policies of what is allowed in making deals. Why not consider tapping into these sales practices for marketing purposes? Used well, they may help you create meaningful promotions.

However, now is not the time to consider how to enhance marketing efforts. Simply focus on what is on the surface at your fingertips and with anyone else on your core strategy team. At this stage, aim to spend no more than fifteen minutes speaking with someone in sales for their insights to affirm or disprove the sales process and relative scripts and standards you have outlined thus far.

Deep interviewing of salespeople in the Gathering Intelligence Data section will help you fill in any gaps where sales process information, scripts, and standards are lacking. For now, let's keep momentum.

> **Guiding Principle:** Knowing what helps move prospects forward from one step to the next through the sales process is important. Only with formal documentation can this become a core tenant of your business, and only then can you truly iterate and improve on the current standards and activities.

1.1.6
Sales & Marketing Collateral

Collateral can refer to any materials that help to educate prospects and keep your company top of mind when you are not in direct communication with a prospect. While this commonly refers to physical items like brochures, this can extend to digital elements, such as sales pages on your website, email newsletters, and premium content such as eBooks, white papers, and guides.

Again, this phase is only focused on collection of what already exists. Organize these items in a central location or create a spreadsheet to track the collateral, as we did with our databases and lists. Remember to note the file name, the content's purpose, what context it is used in, and if it is still relevant or if the content needs updating.

It is helpful to gain feedback on this content from key stakeholders, as well. That can be market experts, such as star salespeople, or customers themselves. This is an "extra" activity at this stage, but it may reveal quite a bit about the quality and relevance of the content that should be educating your audience.

> **Guiding Principle:** Collateral and content should be education-focused. Accordingly, it must align well with what is on the consumers' mind. By taking an inventory of the collateral and content you have, its purpose, and its use case, you can determine what topics appear relevant to your audience.

1.1.7
Customer Experience Maps

To conclude the mining intelligence assets phase, collect any customer experience maps the company has created.

A customer experience map provides a physical, tangible framework for us to understand the consumer experience and buying process. It incorporates everything that customers *Think*, *Feel*, and *Do* across their buying journey and your sales process.

In contrast to the sales process, this is *less about your activities* and *more about your customers'*. This includes their interactions with your company, but extends to their interactions with competitors and ancillary activities that may not include interaction with any company.

Like with market research, we want to be sure that the map is relevant and was created in a strategic, well-thought-out manner. If you are one of the few companies to already have an experience map today, simply validate its quality as you continue.

If you do not have a map now, don't worry about creating one. We will soon, but you can move forward to the next phase without it.

> **Guiding Principle:** Like Buyer Personas, the Customer Experience Map provides a depth to understanding your customers. This illuminates and visualizes everything the customer experiences, allowing you to meet the customer where they are throughout their buying journey.

1.2
GATHER INTELLIGENCE DATA

Think of Intelligence Data as information that supports and supplements the Assets you were able to find.

This part of Phase 1 is more collaborative because to gather data effectively, you must involve other parties. This may include in-house experts, such as salespeople, customer service reps, and executives, or external stakeholders, such as partners, customers, and prospects.

We are looking to tap into the "collective intelligence" of the various internal and external stakeholders to provide us with breadth and depth of insight on your company, your market, and your customers.

You can accomplish this through the following methodical approach. This is the essence of the phase you will now begin.

1.2.1
Marketing Questionnaire

I recommend dedicating time to completing an in-depth questionnaire that compresses all information related to your marketing, advertising, promotion, and sales into a single document. This will become your master document, acting as a cohesive overview of all current marketing protocol. It should also be considered a *live document*, since all materials we develop continually evolve as changes occur. This master document should reflect those changes and iterations.

In this questionnaire, outline the following areas:

- Current responsible and accountable parties
- Basic company information
- Company descriptors
- Value proposition and selling points
- Target market information
- Marketing and technology inventory
- Current digital marketing funnel(s)
- Databases and lists
- Sales processes
- Competitor listing
- Marketing goals: short- and long-term
- Marketing budgets

To provide a complete questionnaire in this book would be excessive, unmanageable, and incomprehensible. Please refer to the bonus resources held in an online repository found here: **DavidJBradley.com/digital-mba-resources/**.

> **Guiding Principle:** Bringing all marketing-related materials into a single document is helpful to develop consistent practices, simplify decision making, and improve training.

1.2.2
Marketing & Technology Inventory

The inventorying activity serves to collect a high-level overview of all existing initiatives and technologies associated with or supporting your marketing, sales and customer service teams, and activities.

To keep this organized, we will create a spreadsheet to document this inventory. I will walk you through the step-by-step creation of this.

The first step of this process is to list *every* program, initiative, or activity that your company has utilized in the last twelve months related to marketing, advertising, sales, customer service, and analytics. Additionally, you should list all technologies related to these fields.

Start your spreadsheet with Column A titled "Programs & Tech." This is where your marketing programs and technologies will be listed. Only proceed forward after naming all relevant subjects.

In the second column, you can now write a one-to-two sentence description of what purpose the program or technology serves to your business *in its existing form*. Again, this inventory is an overview, so it should be able to be absorbed at a glance. Title Column B "Brief Description."

Now, proceeding row by row, identify all software, technology, and tools that make it possible for you to execute the given activity effectively. If reviewing a technology on the list, then identify all other technologies that integrate with it and personnel who maintain the software, if relevant. Title Column C "Database & Tools Used to Execute."

The remaining columns are described below. You can progress through completing the spreadsheet information column by column or row by row, to your preference. If some topics are not relevant to the given activity or technology, you may skip them.

Column D – "Variable Marketing Costs": List what costs are associated with this program and how they are incurred. For example, the costs may be ad spending or list purchases, and they may be incurred by cost per thousand impressions (CPM), cost per click (CPC), or placement costs.

Column E – "Salary, Tech & Overhead Expenses": Calculate the costs of personnel, subscriptions, and any overhead related to this individual program. Typically, costs are displayed on an annual basis.

Column F – "Frequency": Identify how often this initiative is activated. It may be ongoing, daily, weekly, monthly, quarterly, seasonally, ad hoc, or sporadically.

Column G – "Targeting Criteria": Share how you identify the audience targeted by this channel. For example, it may be persona-based, intent-based, existing customers, or from a prior engagement.

Column H – "Audience Size": List the approximate reach you achieve through this marketing initiative. If no specific reach is identified, make note accordingly. If a variable reach is seen, you may list the maximum audience size based on the activity's targeting criteria.

Column I – "Data Sources": List where your data used in this channel or targeting comes from. For example, that may be your own CRM, the platform itself, or a purchased list.

Column J – "KPIs Tracked": What Key Performance Indicators do you use currently to track progress? Do not worry about what they "should be." Simply note *what they are today*.

Column K – "KPIs Untracked": List any relevant KPIs that you do not currently track, regardless of the reason, whether inability or lack of existing protocol. Typical KPIs include return on investment (ROI), return on ad spend (ROAS), cost per lead (CPL), and cost per sale (CPS).

Column L – "Analytics Systems": List any analytics software and tools used with this individual program or integrating with this tech. This could be the platform itself or third-party tools. Again, you may have analytics technologies listed in rows, so you may identify integrating tools or activities in those cases.

Column M – "Response Channel(s)": List any channels customers can use to respond to contacts relative to this program. This may be based on the call-to-action or any contact points they can easily find from this program, such as email, phone, live chat, social media, or store visits.

After completion of all columns and rows, you will have a master document serving as an overview of all existing activities. This is something we will build upon, starting with the next section: Program Gap Assessment.

> **Guiding Principle:** Inventorying your marketing and technology provides you with a simple yet comprehensive informational overview of all facets of your marketing, including those that directly and indirectly affect your activities and decision making.

1.2.3
Program Gap Assessment

The program gap assessment may be developed from the marketing and technology inventory. This is when we assess the programs' strengths, weaknesses, and desired improvements. Again, the collective intelligence from multiple parties directly and indirectly involved in each program or technology is helpful.

With your spreadsheet, populate the next available columns as follows:

Column N – "Strengths of Current Process": Identify all the positives in how the program exists today. This can refer to the process or the provided results. Write qualitative answers in bullet-list format. If it helps to support these answers with quantitative result data correlated with the strengths and benefits, add it.

Column O – "Execution Gaps & Challenges": Identify all problems and issues, large or small. These can be existing or foreseen going forward based upon the technology variations, use case, involved personnel, or business changes.

Column P – "Desired Capabilities": List all desired capabilities that do not exist with the current software or program. This should be treated as a brainstorming session, so make note of each idea without concern to how it would specifically be used. We do not want to limit creative thinking by judging individual desires on any criteria.

Completion of this program gap assessment allows us to understand what we need to capitalize on and improve upon while making decisions related to channels and technologies going forward. It's an exercise for prioritization and insight.

Comparative to the inventory, this activity requires a leader to facilitate discussion. We are seeking an opportunity to learn from the people who use the technologies and execute the activities. This requires an open, collaborative environment where free and honest conversation is possible as these challenges may relate to people involved or decisions previously made that did not or no longer best serve the company.

> **Guiding Principle:** Creating a gap assessment allows you to glean insights from people who use and manage the marketing and technology programs day-to-day to identify existing weaknesses and missing needs.

1.2.4
Competitive Intel

Like it or not, most businesses operate in *red waters*, competing directly with other companies with relatively similar positioning, vying for the same customers.

Let's assume you managed to innovate your business enough to differentiate yourself or you fortunately have no competitors in your market. Competitive intel can still produce findings about what is and is not working in your market, so it is important to conduct a review.

There are several components of competitive intel to investigate:

- Reputation review
- Social media landscape breakdown

- Marketing channel assessment
- Marketing message examination
- Search engine analysis
- Offers and innovations

Before you begin, you need to qualify *who* qualifies as a competitor. While you may have specific competitors in mind, I want you to expand your thinking by viewing competitors through specific lenses. Take out a notepad and make note of your competitors using the proposed perspectives below.

Begin by identifying the industry leader – or the top few if there is not a clear, single leader. It does not matter whether you ever aspire to become the industry leader. We still want to review what they are doing. If they are investing eight or nine figures in marketing every year, we can thank them as we leverage their investment for our own insights.

Now, who are the industry innovators? "Innovators" may make your mind may jump to tech companies first. Don't forget anyone who is reinventing how they *structure* their business or how they reinvented the customer experience. Simple research on innovation news within your industry through word of mouth, press releases, associations, and industry or consumer events may reveal additional findings.

Next, identify three to five of the companies most similar to your company in operations, size, and customer base. These are your most direct competitors, those you most frequently lose customers or opportunities to. Follow this perspective with three to five companies slightly larger than yours, in the next stage of business growth.

Finally, complete the exercise by taking note of who the most admired company is in your industry. If there is one, or a few, that particularly stand out, we want to make note of this and understand why that is. If you don't have an answer instantly, you will likely find out exactly why they are so admired by you or others while conducting the competitive intelligence. The reputation review exercise will often reveal this.

Competitors by Perspective:

- Industry leaders
- Industry innovators
- Direct competitors
- Most admired companies

> **Guiding Principle:** Do not rely on the first competitor or two that comes to mind for competitive intel. We want to create a competitor list that provides different perspectives on the market.

Reputation Review

There is no better way to understand what your customers love *and* hate than seeing their reviews of your company and your competitors.

Depending on your industry, there may be several specific review sites and platforms. To provide you with a starting point, consider reviewing company listings across Google, Better Business Bureau (BBB), Angie's List, ConsumerAffairs, Yelp, and Facebook.

Let's not forget employees. Their reviews of companies often reveal quite a bit about what they deal with internally and how customers are handled. Glassdoor and Indeed are two excellent sources where people review how a company is to work for, in addition to reviewing the leadership.

Remember, you are looking for insights that help you understand how to communicate with your market, what their words are, and what they really care about. What are the hot buttons that show their excitement? What do they get upset about? Take advantage of this resource because it allows you to go directly to the source.

> **Guiding Principle:** Going directly to consumer reviews allows you to understand what excites and frustrates customers, while hearing it *in their own words*. This can be powerful in aligning your company to these joys and pains, as well as for communicating in a familiar language.

Social Media Landscape Breakdown

Before we begin surveying our competitors' social media channels, we need to identify what channels to review. It is safe to assume leading, relevant platforms should be included, such as Facebook, Twitter, and Instagram.

On the surface, this is a low-intensity project, as long as you avoid getting lost down the rabbit hole of social media. Accordingly, I recommend including other leading platforms of relevance, such as LinkedIn, Pinterest, and Snapchat.

Your industry may have additional or niche channels, as well, including message boards and forums. I recommend including two to five of these to make this as comprehensive as possible. Research what is relevant to your target market.

As you go, fill out a spreadsheet with each channel linked for each competitor, their followers count, and an estimation of their relative activity on that channel compared to the industry in general. You may label this as a relative judgment such as "Low, Medium, High," or a numerical scale such as "X Posts Daily," for example. The goal is simplicity in execution and comprehension in later reviewing the research so that you can clearly identify the most active channels across different competitors.

> **Guiding Principle:** Social media is an important element of business today, but companies utilize it in many ways (branding, lead generation, customer service, for example). Understand how your competitors use it, but do not assume their methods are according to best practices or are a fit for yours. Simply observe.

Marketing Channel Assessment

With social media channels recorded, expand your analysis to address other marketing channels used by competitors.

If you can gain insight on offline marketing activities as well, I would encourage you to do so. Online and offline channels are stronger when integrated together.

There is a list of channels to consider below. Again, record any learnings you can from each channel – whether that is regarding their approximate reach, notes on how you can review this channel again in the future, frequency of channel use, and so on:

- Trade shows
- Direct mail
- Email newsletters
- Automated email series
- Content marketing
- Search advertising
- Social advertising
- Community building
- Public relations
- Display advertising
- Retargeting/remarketing
- Influencer marketing
- Affiliate/ambassador programs
- Radio advertising
- TV advertising
- Offline events

Much of this investigation requires dedicating time into research. There are no shortcuts, but you will learn a lot along the way. Additionally, you cannot expect to get answers for every tactic, as some may be hidden from public view or are ad hoc/sporadic on their part.

Remember to make it easy to refer back to this information, whether that means noting where information is stored on the competitors' channel or linking directly to webpages that provide more information on the given competitor and channel.

This overview will become a resource we can tap into in the future as we plan specific campaigns and strategies and wish to glean insights from our competitors and how they have handled different initiatives.

For now, keep information binary: *do they use search advertising, yes or no?* If yes, and if you know how to quickly find approximate monthly spend or reach, add the relevant data. If you don't have this information available, move on. We can return to find these details in the strategy development phase, where you may consider investing more time and money in your team finding the information or in contracting an expert to help assess certain areas of your research.

> **Guiding Principle:** Cross-channel assessment of activities provides you with an opportunity to tap into the successes and progresses of your competitors. This can be particularly insightful in bridging the gap between the offline and online world.

Marketing Message Examination

Now that you have thoroughly identified marketing channels, examine the marketing messages communicated by each competitor across each channel. Headlines tell us a lot, as they are (or should be) "attention-getters." You can start there for ease of research.

Smaller competitors may not be sophisticated enough to determine if that attention-getter is aligned to the market, but often large enterprises who dedicate many millions each year will have a well-refined message backed by data. You may not blindly accept these headlines as proven and applicable to you, but we can save them for future testing.

Extending beyond the headline, make note of the value proposition and selling points proposed in the copy itself. Note how the messaging attempts to position the product, service or company to the market. The company's homepage and the associated calls-to-action will provide further insight in what they tell the market and ask for them to do to initiate a "next step" between the company and the customer.

The final materials from this examination will help us to determine what commonalities exist and can help us not only identify what we could say, but how we can stand out with our messaging in the future.

> **Guiding Principle:** Similar to reviewing what consumers say, observing the language competing marketing initiatives incorporate may inform you of angles that you can leverage or counteract.

Search Engine Analysis

Analyzing your competitors' search engine optimization strategies allows you to determine strengths and weaknesses compared to your brand, helping you to determine your own strategy. With SEO, not every battle is worth fighting, so to be successful, you need to identify what are the easiest and best-fitting wins you can pursue. This analysis will help you do that.

Search analysis is one-part user experience based (think fast page loading, ease of finding relevant information, and overall site friendliness) and one-part technical audit (think content indexed with search engines, not ranking for desired terms/keywords, and poor presentation in search).

This would be an appropriate time to conduct an SEO analysis on your own website to determine problem areas and comparative standing, so include your business in this analysis.

To provide a full "how to" in this book would not be possible – or very helpful in this format. Nevertheless, I recommend hiring an SEO specialist who can conduct this research for you. A specialist will help you maintain momentum on strategy development while providing greater quality, unless you have a well-versed team member in SEO audits.

As with any hire, split test them, as I will explain in Phase 3 of this book.

> **Guiding Principle:** A search engine analysis will reveal what your competitors are doing to appear in search queries that customers use in their buying journey. This is composed of the user experience and the technical structure of the website.

Offers & Innovations

In Phase 2 (Strategy Development), we are going to look deeper into what our online value proposition is and how we can innovate the customer experience. To support this planning, we need to prepare by conducting relevant research.

Review what each company is *offering* to the market and *how* they have innovated the customer experience, whether that is how customers evaluate the company, find a solution, make a purchase, or use the product.

Documentation of this across competitors is helpful to spur creativity and ensure exclusivity of value propositions and experiences in the next phase. To creatively disrupt, you need to be armed with both information and inspiration.

> **Guiding Principle:** An offer made into the market is a high leverage variable to test across marketing and advertising. Accordingly, seeing the offers and language used across competitors may help you to brainstorm your own offers or alternatives. Likewise, innovating the customer experience can drastically transform your business and opportunities.

1.2.5
Interviewing Key Stakeholders

This is my favorite part of the entire Market Intelligence phase. You connect with many stakeholders, gleaning insights from a variety of perspectives, while gaining their buy-in to this process. This can be a transformational experience. Additionally, I recommend you make it an ongoing activity.

You need to invest time in customizing questions to fit your audience – whether an internal employee, external partner, or a won or lost customer. Between the audience types, questions typically remain relatively consistent in the intent of what they ask, but the structure may change. I will provide you with an example interview guide to help you get started in the book resources.

Begin by identifying three members from each internal audience: sales, marketing, customer service, and company leadership. Additionally, two partners by each classification of partner type, such as strategic alliances, consultants, and vendors that serve you. Focus on those who have established or recent relationships with your company *and* your competitors.

After speaking with those employees and partners, continue on to speak with approximately eight to ten customers. If you can speak with lost customers who decided to go with a competitor, that will provide excellent insight, as well.

Each type of customer will have their own interview guide with slightly different questions. This will be even easier to develop after your employee and partner interviews conclude.

Note: I often send customer participants a gift card as a thank you for their time.

You may conduct 20-25 interviews total. This is a lot. If we assume a half hour average per interview, this would require ten to twelve focused hours. Also consider that customer interviews may extend to 45-60 minutes, potentially resulting in an additional five hours.

However, with careful scheduling, you can complete this within two weeks. And, I believe this to be the single most powerful activity in strategically reviewing your company, including and beyond digital. It is well worth the investment.

Make sure that these interviews are recorded. Have them transcribed afterwards, allowing you to focus entirely on the conversation itself, rather than taking notes. While you may have a scribe join you, I find that one-on-one conversations often provide deeper and more honest insight.

Your first step is to adequately explain *why* you are conducting these interviews and *how* the interviewee will contribute to what you are seeking to accomplish: *the vision*. If recording, be clear about that, share why, and request their consent.

For internal stakeholders and partners, the interview covers the individual's connection to customers, opinions about the company's position in the market, the competitive landscape, company policies, and customers' motivations towards or away from the company.

For customers, won and lost, the conversation takes a different approach. Internal audiences focus on the company, competitors, and the market. We want to understand as much as possible about the *buyer's journey*, starting from the initial moment they faced a problem. This journey extends to the point of purchase and beyond, including product or service use, customer service, referrals, repeat buys, loyalty programming, and anything else post-purchase.

Customers can provide us with insights on each stage of the buying process, from how they made decisions to what they thought and felt. This conversation can get personal and should not be limited to their interactions with your company alone. You want to know as much as possible about their journey outside of their interactions with you.

At the conclusion, always thank them for their time and let them know of next steps. If you will be able to share findings with them, you provide them with added certainty that they invested their time well, they are valued, and that this is not a throw-away conversation. If you will not be able to share, explain that their insights will be helpful in shaping an improved customer experience.

After completing interviews, have conversations transcribed so you can more easily review the talks and extract insights. Organizing insights by question asked will help you to compile findings and seek out common themes across different parties.

You will be amazed at the thoughts and ideas generated from this activity. The amount of education gained will transform how you think about your business, customers, and marketing. This activity provides much of the insight you need to develop a buyer persona – which we will address soon.

Note: I recommend you make this a regular practice. Each month, schedule time to talk with two or three customers. Keep your finger on the pulse. Information is a competitive advantage.

> **Guiding Principle:** The depth of insight you can garner from interviewing stakeholders cannot be matched with quantitative research, big data, or industry reports. Invest the time with these stakeholders for the greatest business education you can receive.

1.2.6
Focus Groups

I firmly believe in collecting qualitative data prior to quantitative data, which is why I suggest key stakeholder interviews first.

The findings from these interviews help you to form educated hypotheses about your market and business operations. You can continue your investigation by proving or disproving hypotheses through focus groups or surveying, if you wish. We will begin by examining focus groups.

Again, there are three primary parties you can extract insights from: internal experts, external partners, and customers. Each may have their own focus group.

I cannot provide you with a guide on what questions to ask because ideally, you can easily create one yourself as an iteration of your key stakeholder interviews and the findings from them. This exercise allows you to dive deeper into conversations and facilitate a back-and-forth exchange of thoughts.

Here are some points to consider when planning your focus groups:

- Parties most needed for insights
- Who will serve as moderators and scribes
- Participant information forms on registration
- Informed consent forms on registration
- Categories of discussion
- Questions per category
- Thank you gifts for participation

Aside from logistics, much of your effort is in deciding the categories of discussion and questions for each category. Aim for three to five categories and three to five questions per category. This allows you to be flexible and let discussions flow naturally, while still maintaining focus on your intended topics.

Focus groups can be helpful, but it is at your discretion whether this is needed based on information gathered to date.

> **Guiding Principle:** Use focus groups to test hypotheses formed through key stakeholder interviews. If professionally managed for depth of discussion and avoidance of groupthink, they can be greatly informative.

1.2.7
Mass Surveying

Surveying may serve as an alternative to focus groups for proving or disproving hypotheses, or it can be an exercise to follow focus groups. This works particularly well if you have database lists available.

Surveys operate in a similar function to focus groups, but utilize a different channel. You may also elect to present the same questions in a different way to determine if language dictates a certain answer or perspective.

Again, the need of this exercise is at your discretion. It certainly can help, but there are costs in time to develop and interpret results. Time goes into developing questions, designing the survey, distribution, waiting for responses, and the interpreting results. You must determine if it is worthwhile based on the costs and iterative gains.

> **Guiding Principle:** Surveying provides scale you cannot achieve through interviews or focus groups. This process is aided if you have databases of relevant contacts to distribute questions to. This is another method to prove or disprove hypotheses from stakeholder interviews.

1.2.8
Buyer Persona Development

We previously discussed buyer personas and how they represent your customers' demographics, online behavior, personal histories, motivations, and concerns.

At this stage, if you have conducted the interviews, you should be capable of effectively designing a buyer persona. This should serve as a "living document," evolving as you continue to learn. Nonetheless, the amount of information collected to date should be sufficient for a strong foundation, particularly if paired with focus groups or survey findings.

Below is my recommended buyer persona format, which formed from Jill Konrath's methodology in *SNAP Selling* (2012). You can download a cleaner version in the book's resources, as well.

- Persona name
- First-person one-liner: "I am a ..."
- Persona background briefing
- High-level persona breakdown:
    - Personal goals
    - Personal objectives
    - External challenges
    - Buying strategies
    - Primary interfaces
    - Change drivers
- Social/online communities
- Questions and pains at awareness stage
- Questions and pains at consideration stage
- Questions and pains at decision stage

Completion of a buyer persona is one of the most powerful creations for your company from this process. It can be used to educate, train, and improve cohesion of the company and brand across departments and seniority levels.

To create this, begin completing the outline based on what you know of the market from your customers' perspective. Use their own language, which was found in your research thus far. If you get stuck or are uncertain on any element, make note and keep going. You have a stable of helpers you can revisit if you need help gaining clarity and certainty: your internal experts, external partners, and customers. Again, this is a living document, so perfection is not the objective.

> **Guiding Principle:** Create a buyer persona. It provides a basis for directing all communications to the market, every message and activity, to one individual: the buyer persona. Your teams become more efficient, your branding consistent, and your marketing more effective.

PHASE 1 CONCLUSION

You can consider this phase completed by checking off a few milestones in your journey:

Mined Intelligence Assets:

- Collection of market research
- Identification, sourcing, and cleansing of databases
- Collection of buyer personas
- Identification of sales processes
- Collection of sales scripts and standards
- Collection of sales and marketing collateral
- Identification of customer experience maps

Gathered Intelligence Data:

- Answered marketing questionnaire
- Inventoried marketing programs and technologies
- Assessed program gaps
- Conducted competitive intel
- Interviewed key stakeholders
- Conducted focus groups
- Surveyed audiences
- Developed buyer persona(s)

If you have addressed everything above – or at least the most fitting activities – congratulations. You have far more depth and breadth of understanding than most, or all, direct competitors will have, and you can use this as a competitive advantage, deciding to outthink instead of outspend competition.

That was most of the heavy lifting. You can now continue to Phase 2: Strategy Development. In this phase, we will take our findings and discoveries and make data-backed decisions on communication channels, processes, and technologies.

PHASE 2
STRATEGY DEVELOPMENT

Now things get more exciting. The Strategy Development phase is our first steps to solidifying *how* we engage the market through digital.

This phase has two core components: reviewing processes and technology, and selecting communication channels. This is what gives sustenance and structure to your digital activities.

Beyond a channel strategy, we will consider how digital changes the business model and the customers' experience. We will clearly define and redevelop our customers' digital experience's purpose and processes.

While channels may appear obvious – online advertising, content marketing, social media marketing – actual pursuit of individual channels require individual strategies, inter-channel integration, and prioritization based on resources and business value.

This book provides a process, but it is not meant to be *entirely* linear. This is particularly relevant in this section. You may wish to revisit one element after reviewing another. For example, the upcoming development of your digital touchpoints and customer experience map might change how you view your online value proposition. Follow the process, but stay flexible.

2.1
REVIEW PROCESSES & TECHNOLOGY

Before we plan *how* we will market ourselves online, we should step back to reconsider the experiences we provide today and how we may improve and evolve going forward. With the effort going into this digital strategy process, capitalize on the moment to make significant improvements to your business. Seek out the 10x transformations, rather than the 10% iterations.

Remember that we are restructuring our business to align with our consumers' behavior. The information previously collected will show you how your consumers behave today. *Align to your customers.*

2.1.1
Online Value Proposition

You are familiar with *value propositions* – a unique, special characteristic, offer, or way of doing business that makes a company stand out in the market.

I'm asking you to now identify potential value propositions you can offer the market, but with specific thought to digital – the online experience.

An online value proposition can be relative to products, services or special offers that can only be claimed online. It can take the form of redefining how customers interact with your company, such as offering an option to review their account online, rather than by calling in. It could be for prospects to get an instant quote online, rather than having to talk with a salesperson.

You should employ your own creativity, as well as leveraging insights from interviews previously conducted. A few questions you may ask yourself to focus on relevant areas of consideration are:

- How can we change how we deliver our product?
- How can we offer more value with our existing product?
- How can we repackage our product for digital delivery?
- How can we offer digital interactions in the existing buyer's journey?
- How can we make the buying process faster and easier through digital?
- How can we operate more efficiently or effectively by leveraging digital?

Begin with a volume of ideas. Focus on quantity over quality, allowing for free and creative thinking. Then, narrow down ideas by removing those that are lower quality, based upon these criteria:

- Value to the customers
- Value to the company
- Ease of implementation
- Costs to integrate the proposed idea

It is not necessary to decide on a single online value proposition. If appropriate and manageable, consider all that will allow you to add additional value *or* as many as you can reasonably test to find what is optimal.

> **Guiding Principle:** Brainstorm ways to offer unique value to the market through digital means. Start with quantity of ideas before concerning yourself with feasibility or maximal value. Narrow your ideas by set criteria: value to customers, value to the company, ease of implementation, and associated costs.

2.1.2
Digital Touchpoints

Mapping out the touchpoints your customers and prospects experience online will help you to identify weaknesses and opportunities.

A touchpoint is any moment of interaction with your brand. That can be as simple as viewing a website, where no direct communication is taking place.

You are looking to determine touchpoints that *exist*, *do not exist*, and that *can be improved*. You may even discover that a touchpoint should be removed due to redundancy or lack of added-value.

After identifying and classifying touchpoints, review them to measure message consistency, or inconsistency, across various touches.

Use the diagram provided on the following page to help you identify all relevant areas.

Shallow

- ☐ Name
- ☐ Headline
- ☐ Online product design
- ☐ Website content
- ☐ Pricing model
- ☐ Display advertising
- ☐ Social networks
- ☐ Industry news sites
- ☐ Local news sites
- ☐ Product placement

- ☐ Blogging
- ☐ Newsletters
- ☐ Social media marketing
- ☐ Testimonials/ratings
- ☐ Website navigation
- ☐ Digital point of sale
- ☐ Mobile apps
- ☐ Automated follow-ups
- ☐ Loyalty program
- ☐ Customer service via email
- ☐ Sales pitches
- ☐ Product demos
- ☐ Online communities

General ──────────────────── **Personal**

- ☐ Thought leadership
- ☐ Partnerships
- ☐ Welcome packet
- ☐ Public appearances
- ☐ Community givebacks
- ☐ Sponsorships

- ☐ Live chat
- ☐ Customer service via social
- ☐ Online product/service use
- ☐ Customer reviews
- ☐ Webinars
- ☐ Customer events
- ☐ Influencer marketing
- ☐ Search engine presence
- ☐ Social media advertising

Deep

Guiding Principle: Identify touchpoints that exist, do not exist, can be improved, and can be removed. Check for consistency of messaging during this exercise. This is focused on identification of to-dos, not projects to undertake immediately, so hold on to these notes for Phase 3.

2.1.3
Digital Marketing Funnels

A digital marketing funnel is the online process that you build to move a prospective customer from first contact to the point-of-sale.

To provide further context, funnels typically have traffic driven to them from advertising channels, such as Google or Facebook. Funnels feature landing pages to capture contact information and ongoing communications to nurture the prospects.

For purposes of this section, we only need to review the marketing funnel concept, rather than be concerned with creating funnels. Funnel creation is part of the channel strategy, as each individual channel may have its own funnel to guide prospects through, or a multi-channel funnel may be developed. But before we create, we must understand best practice.

From a high-level view, there are three core stages of the funnel:

Stage 1: How Traffic Is Driven

Stage 2: How Traffic Is Converted to Leads

Stage 3: How Leads Are Converted to Sales

Stage 1 will be dependent on your channel strategy. Stage 3 is dependent on your sales process. I will share principles I believe in relative to Stage 2, where landing pages are planned, designed, and developed.

Proper design of landing pages and "thank you" pages is a common yet specialized topic, so I will not exhaustively invest your time into studying it here. If you are unfamiliar, a quick Google search will help you identify the proper structure of each.

The three most important principles for landing pages (and thank you pages):

1. Consistency between the ad/source and the page.
2. Simplicity is often best. Less can be more.
3. A single call-to-action is all they want.

I will briefly explain each principle for further clarity:

Landing Page Principle One: Consistency

People respond well to patterns. Interrupt a pattern, and you will halt their momentum. Pattern interruptions can be helpful in the right context, but in a funnel, we want to make it as easy and clear as possible *how* to continue forward.

Consistency in messaging and visuals helps to avoid interruptions.

- Click on an ad from one brand and end up on another brand's website? It happens – and it hurts the campaign.
- Click on an ad based on one headline and land on a page with different messaging? That may throw you off.
- Click on an ad to download an eBook and land on a page with a 3D version of an eBook cover prominently displayed? *"Yes, I'm in the right place!"*

Landing pages allow us opportunities to test, which is a great benefit. Before you follow the latest hype article about how changing one word in your headline will triple conversions, find baseline performance by creating consistency between traffic source and landing page messaging and visuals.

Landing Page Principle Two: Simplicity

Information is helpful...until it isn't. One of the most common issues I have found with landing pages is that *they try too hard*, adding more graphics and text than is helpful.

This is subject to the market and use case, but again, testing can reveal quite a bit of information. You may test a "long form" landing page with a number of testimonials, selling points, and product information. Then, compare it to a short, to-the-point landing page that presents only the headline, offer, and opt-in form. Compare results.

I have seen clients find great results from landing pages with a single headline, one image, and a form requesting name and email. In one case, the conversion rate was 58% from cold Facebook Advertising traffic. This was more than double the performance of the long-form variant.

Landing page architecture is counterintuitive, but simple. Instead of offering everything the prospect could possibly want to know, offer as little information as needed to be understood and for them to move forward.

Note: It's always important to also consider lead quality, not simply lead quantity. That carries weight, as ten leads who will buy are more profitable than a thousand leads who will never buy. The true best-fit is often somewhere in the middle.

Landing Page Principle Three: Singular Focus

If you are familiar with landing pages and "calls-to-action," then you probably know the concept of using a single CTA on the page.

Having singular focus is the third principle because of its efficacy. People respond best when they have fewer decisions and options. Additionally, you are better able to control the complete experience with fewer possible avenues for the customer.

With only one focus on the page, the process simplifies for both your prospects and your marketing team as they continue to develop the marketing funnel.

> **Guiding Principle:** Digital marketing funnels are a framework to ensure that there is a natural flow for consumers to move through: from first touch, to engaging, to follow-up. In digital, landing pages are helpful to provide simple next steps that keep a new prospect engaged and interested. Keep these pages *consistent, simple,* and *focused.*

2.1.4
Customer Experience Innovations

Customer experience maps allow you to determine impacts and innovations your company can offer to the market while optimizing existing activities across marketing, sales, and customer service functions. This is a systematic and strategic way of deepening your understanding of customers: what makes them tick, their purchasing patterns, and the impacts and innovations you can make on them that leads to exponential growth.

You can begin this process with a diagnosis, physically mapping out the customer experience. This includes stages of the buying process, outlining channels used to communicate with the customers throughout, and beginning an understanding of what the customers *Do, Think,* and *Feel* at each stage.

For help with determining what stages exist, and what customers experience at each stage, you can refer back to the stakeholder interviews you conducted, as well as any other helpful information you have collected.

Here are some examples of how Customer Experience Map stages may be defined:

- General: awareness, consideration of options, pricing and quotes, purchase, product use, loyalty program
- B2B: research, compare, quote, sign-off, partnership
- B2C: identify need, search for options, discuss with friends, make first order, await delivery, use item
- Travel industry: trip planning, shopping, booking, pre-travel, travel, post-travel

The result of this will be a detailed framework that can be enhanced over time. The map will reveal innovative and unique ways to augment the process, making it easier for customers to buy, to pique interest and excitement at different stages, to answer questions and concerns along the journey, and to translate these feelings and thoughts into initial sales and repeat buys.

Innovating on the existing map is further supported by research done throughout the Market Intelligence phase, including what competitors are offering to their customers. Tap into these notes to brainstorm your own ideas of how to better serve the market.

The focus of this process should be to improve the customer experience: customer-centric innovations. Sometimes, this means increasing sales cycles or conversions from prospect to buyer or both. The result may be exponential growth through a tangible innovation process.

> **Guiding Principle:** Design a customer experience map that highlights the thoughts, feelings, and actions through each stage of the buying journey. Use this map to determine where shortcomings and opportunities exist within the maps' gaps or existing elements of the customer experience.

2.1.5
Customer Loyalty Programming

Existing customers are often the highest leverage aspect of a business for growth. There is a tremendous amount of potential to tap into if you carefully consider better ways to develop and amplify loyalty among your customer base.

Traditionally, loyalty programs were simple, straightforward, and often, lackluster. You buy, you earn points, you redeem the points.

A more holistic view on loyalty programming allows you to develop and deepen relationships from a variety of angles. You simply must align yourself to what customers truly care about and are incentivized by.

People love to be recognized. Opportunities for recognition come when a customer is a frequent user of your product, provides a testimonial, or refers your business. Simply highlighting them among your community – such as in message boards, on your blog, at events, or through email – can leave a lasting impact and deepen that loyalty. Making this a process in your organization *is* loyalty programming.

Additional rewards for use of your product can be helpful, too. Gamification of product use has become more common. You may accomplish this through partnerships with other companies, providing a special offer from the partners to your customer base.

Rewards can also be contained to your company alone. Again, aligning to what your customers would consider a real and worthwhile reward is paramount. Then, build the process.

Exclusivity is what the entire luxury goods industry is based upon because there is a special magnetism to it. You can use that in your loyalty program, providing exclusive features, content, products, or services to your most loyal customers.

The way someone collects points or bonuses is through their loyalty. This may be through vocal support of your company, subscribing for a monthly subscription, using your product, or through additional purchases.

The deeper and stronger your relationship with existing customers is, the faster you will see revenues increase and the more valuable each additional new customer becomes.

> **Guiding Principle:** Determine ways to build loyalty programming into your model. Before worrying about the technical execution, consider what options exist. Think back to your competitive intel and whether any competitors offer special incentives for customers in their marketing. Start with what customers will find real and relevant value in, and then develop the processes and programming.

2.1.6
Marketing Technology (MarTech)

Marketing technology, commonly referred to as "MarTech," is the technology that supports your planning, organization, databases, campaigns, and analytics.

Changes to technology platforms in large organizations that span the company, such as CRMs, may require months or years of development. However, smaller organizations can be more agile and isolated tools can provide enhancements to marketing efforts without changing other technologies. In other words, technology decisions, while often offering significant opportunities, range in approach and require a "pick your battles" mindset.

Tech doesn't have to be perfect. I'm not looking to disregard its importance. However, aiming to find the *perfect* technology stack will require a tremendous amount of resources and likely dissipate focus with little return on your investment of time, talent and treasure. Find something that fits the absolute essentials of what is necessary and 80% of nice-to-have features. That is plenty fitting enough.

If you have external technology partners or agencies that are incorporated into the technology use, you will want to consider how agile you can remain with these external forces. Being agile is a philosophy that needs to be embraced by all relevant parties, internal and external.

A complete overview of the Marketing Technology Landscape is provided by Scott Brinker of Chiefmartec.com. Here is a bullet-list form of the categories Brinker provides:

Advertising & Promotion

- Mobile marketing
- Display and programmatic advertising
- Search and social advertising
- Native/content advertising
- Video advertising
- Print
- PR

Content & Experience

- Mobile apps
- Video marketing
- Interactive content
- Email marketing
- Content marketing
- Optimization, personalization, and testing
- DAM and MRM
- SEO

- Marketing automation and campaign/lead management
- CMS and web experience management

Social & Relationships

- Call analytics and management
- Account-based marketing
- Events, meetings, and webinars
- Social media marketing and monitoring
- Advocacy, loyalty, and referrals
- Influencers
- Feedback and chat
- Community and reviews
- Experience, service, and success
- CRMs

Commerce & Sales

- Retail and proximity marketing
- Channel, partner, and local marketing
- Sales automation, enablement, and intelligence
- Affiliate marketing and management
- Ecommerce marketing
- Ecommerce platforms and carts

Data

- Audience/market data and data enhancement
- Marketing analytics, performance, and attribution

- Mobile and web analytics
- Dashboards and data visualization
- Business/customer intelligence and data science
- iPaaS, cloud/data integration and tag management
- Data management platforms
- Predictive analytics
- Customer data platforms

Management

- Talent management
- Product management
- Budgeting and finance
- Collaboration
- Projects and workflow
- Agile and lean management
- Vendor analysis

Explaining the purpose and use case of each of these would be exhaustive and a separate book in and of itself, but I will provide an overview of the most common categories to consider for most businesses.

12 Common Marketing Technologies to Consider

In evaluating tools, there are a few core considerations I recommend:

- How will this integrate with the other technologies we use?
- How reliable is this vendor?
- What support will we have available to use from the vendor?
- What is the learning curve or ease of use like with this product?
- Are we fulfilling all of our identified current and short-term needs?

These criteria will help you to avoid being swayed by poor-fit technologies that offer exciting, but unnecessary features for your business today and in the coming 24 months.

1. Customer Relationship Management (CRM)

CRMs are commonplace in business, but the *right* CRM is an important consideration. There are many tools that offer a CRM, as well as email marketing and marketing automation features. However, you need to determine the features you need, which may have been previously determined in the program and technology gap assessment.

This tool is commonly used by sales teams, but if your marketing and sales are working in tandem, as they should, both teams must make this decision.

2. Email Marketing & Marketing Automation

Email marketing alone is rarely sufficient for today's businesses. Marketing automation, in my opinion, has encompassed and exceeded email marketing providers, while maintaining costs.

In other words, while evaluating an email marketing provider, consider focusing on a well-fit marketing automation tool. You will likely find all you need, while gaining additional features with fewer platforms and more options for features to "grow into" as your marketing becomes more comprehensive and sophisticated.

3. Sales Automation, Enablement & Intelligence

Well-meaning marketers with successful campaigns can often leave salespeople with a pile of leads and no direction on how to approach the overwhelming amount. Lead scoring is one feature of sales automation that often catches the attention of salespeople.

With lead scoring, you can identify criterion that provide positive or negative "points" based upon online behaviors. In other words, the more engaged a prospect is, and as they self-identify as a warm lead based on their behavior, they are provided more points, resulting in a score. Salespeople can use the scores to prioritize leads and follow-up on warm contacts.

4. Search & Social Advertising

Tools selected for this are dependent upon your channel strategy and needs. Most channels will provide their own tools, but you may require additional support for advanced insights, better collaboration, or more efficient processes. Consider how to better equip your advertising teams for success.

5. Social Media Marketing & Monitoring

Like with search and social advertising tools, what you select in this category is dependent on the channels you use and how you approach them. In a general sense, you will run into technology that helps you plan and generate social media content, as well as tools to help you *monitor* your brand across social media and what the market says about you.

6. Feedback & Chat

Improving the customer experience always depends on the customer perspective, so providing avenues for prospects and customers to quickly and easily communicate is important. It may increase sales conversions, too. Live chats provide this and can be an excellent addition for websites to increase sales, retention, and customer satisfaction.

7. Mobile Marketing

There is a great opportunity in the market to incorporate text messages and voicemail drops into marketing campaigns. If you run a mobile app company, as you can imagine, the mobile marketing opportunities expand exponentially. For most businesses, however, there is great power in simply tapping into the super computers that we all carry with us all day, every day. Seek opportunities to use this channel based on your funnels and customer experience map.

8. Search Engine Optimization (SEO)

While search engines continue to evolve, it's important for us to evolve with them. SEO tools can help us to conduct research periodically, as well as monitoring rankings, competitors, and keywords.

If you elect to implement a comprehensive search engine optimization plan, you will want to track the results. SEO tools are useful in planning, execution, and tracking.

9. CMS & Web Experience Management

The "CMS" is your content management system. In other words, it is the platform your website is built upon. This is important to consider based upon what functions you need of your website, particularly as you develop a more sophisticated digital strategy and consider new online value propositions.

Typically, I recommend open platforms that provide a large amount of flexibility and support, such as WordPress. Closed platforms and "proprietary software" offered by some web development firms cause more concern than benefit in most situations. Always maintain ownership of your digital assets and consider flexibility if technology needs change.

10. Optimization, Personalization & Testing

The next evolution of today's marketing will be deeper personalization. While this brings rise to privacy concerns, there are plenty of tools that are not negligent with privacy while providing personalized experiences that perform better than alternatives.

As a basic start to this, landing page builders can help with campaign execution across different channels, rather than developing landing pages directly on the website. These builders provide speed, efficiency, and deep analytics for marketing teams.

11. Call Analytics

If your phones are ringing, particularly for service-based businesses, call tracking can reveal a lot about call performance. In addition to tracking call sources, you may record phone calls, track how long calls last, determine when calls come in, and identify missed calls.

These insights can provide a company with valuable information, allowing them to identify areas of improvement, training needs, and reasoning for poor performance with simple fixes.

12. Collaboration Tools

With so much activity in your digital processes, keeping organized is important. Collaboration tools allow you to do that, whether for internal projects or customer-based campaigns.

As you can see, marketing technology can quickly become overwhelming with the number of categories to consider and the hundreds of tools within each category to evaluate. However, with careful consideration of your priorities, you can begin identifying where to focus attention and what qualifies or disqualifies vendors from consideration.

> **Guiding Principle:** Marketing technology continues to grow in depth and breadth of coverage. Always focus on the highest leverage and best-fit technologies for your company today and where you see it growing in the next 24 months.

2.1.7
Evaluating Your Website As Your Central Hub

It would be negligent for me to skip discussing your website and the main considerations of it. Your website is your central hub of all activities as your campaigns, technologies, and organic exposure often connect back to your website.

Technologically speaking, smaller companies should focus on CMS platforms, web hosts, and templated website themes that are highly supported and independent. The criteria for these vendors then would be a large customer base and a proven track record of quality customer service.

Furthermore, they should not come with any handcuffs, so look over the local web design and hosting agency that wants you to use their "proprietary" custom-developed CMS, rather than WordPress, where nearly 25% of the web is housed.

Choose a web host that provides quality customer service and high loading speeds with technicians on-call (or live chat) who can assist you on demand. If you are using a theme template, make sure its developers have a large customer base and direct channel for support so that you know they are here to stay. If working with a web agency, they should use these criteria, as well.

Making a website *look* nice is easy. Ensuring that the components perform well in the short-term and continue to work together long-term is what we want to focus on. That's risk management.

For mid-sized and large organizations, you need a custom-tailored approach to the website platforms. Again, attractive design is easy; our focus must be on performance.

Marketing-wise, first consider the importance and potential financial returns of redeveloping your website. Depending on the size of your website, the size of your company, the features needed on your site, and content updates, the prices can go from a few thousand to hundreds of thousands for a good website (or millions for major brands).

Make this decision with data. How much revenue did your website contribute to your business last year? Does it appear that this will change in the year ahead? Look at the total traffic to the website and what the conversion rate is from visitor-to-sale. If you can generate 50% more sales online, will it yield more revenue than the cost of updating your website?

As another rule of thumb, there's a good chance that if your website is more than three years old and was not expertly designed with a marketer's mind, you can realize this increase. That makes the financial decision clearer.

But how is the construction of your website today? Typically, there are three issues:

1. Lack of true mobile-responsiveness
2. Poor navigation
3. Inadequate on-site SEO

If you can have these factors evaluated and two of the three fails, that is another sign it may be valuable to redevelop your website.

The actual decisioning process for creating a new website is complex, but what is important here is that we are not concerned with design. We are concerned with what is friendly to the user.

If restructuring the website can make it easier to navigate and find the right information or take that next step forward in the Buyer's Journey, then it may yield a large increase in revenue.

> **Guiding Principle:** Your website is the central hub to your online experience, so invest in it wisely. Sleek design is easy today; you need to prioritize function over form. Nevertheless, find data to support whether an update would provide financial returns.

2.2
SELECT COMMUNICATION CHANNELS

Marketing conversations typically fall back to discussing channels: *how will we reach our customers?* Channel selection and strategies are important, of course. However, they are but one element of the overall marketing strategy and are dependent upon other factors, such as those we worked through in Phase 1.

Nonetheless, we are here! Below are two primary online communication channels that represent a "pull" and a "push" approach, respectively. Each channel and the sub-channels have their own benefits and drawbacks individually and as a system, interrelated to each other. Our goal is to decide which are most relevant to our audience, feasible based on our resources, and wise to pursue based on gathered intelligence data.

I won't tell you *"this is what social media marketing is."* I will, however, provide you with philosophies to approach each channel. There are plenty of free resources online and paid training and coaching providers available who can help with *how-to* guides and execution. Besides, each channel would require its own book for proper and meaningful training.

Finally, as a reminder, this book is about developing your marketing mind as a leader in the digital age. You will know the channel use case, best practices, and selection criteria. You need not learn the execution. That's for your teams to handle.

2.2.1
Pull: Content Marketing

Content marketing is the creation, distribution, and promotion of valuable materials. These materials may come in written, audio or video form.

For simplicity's sake and to align with my philosophical hierarchy of channels, I incorporate several subchannels into "content marketing," in addition to the most obvious such as blogging, video marketing, and podcasts. This includes social media marketing, database and email marketing, community development, and search engine optimization.

Written, Audio & Video Content

Content creation is at the core of content marketing. Quality content must fulfill *at least* one of three purposes: to educate, to engage, or to entertain.

Educating is helpful because it provides direct value to your viewer. Furthermore, it may help that individual make better use of your product, become a repeat customer, or clarify their own need to work with you. This is accomplished by creating content with the focus on helping the customer with the problem they face, with no hidden agenda.

Engaging is less clear, but it is simple: to garner interest and focused attention from an individual. This is particularly true if you can move them to a place of participation with you, the company, or a community of their peers that you have developed. People who feel relevant to others are more engaged and connected, resulting in a deepened relationship. It is innate in people, as always, to thrive on relationships, despite the world being so digitally-focused.

Entertaining can be risky, but also can be highly rewarding by making your company feel personable, relatable and authentic. People have bonded over laughter consistently over the millennia. Follow the basic ground rules you would on a first date (if you want a second): no politics and no religion. Handled well, entertainment is what allows a company to transcend "marketing messages" and become a part of the consumers' life.

The actual form of this educational, engaging, and entertaining contact may be written, audio, or video. For written content, you would primarily consider blogging. However, this may include database and email marketing, search engine optimization, and social media marketing, which we will address shortly.

Furthermore, written content does *not* have to be exclusive to your website. While helpful to have your own blog, you can tap into the networks of others by contributing content to their website or blog. This can be a tremendous help to build your own audience. It opens you to new audiences while providing you with an "endorsement" from the website themselves for having you contribute.

Here's an example of how to use contributing to others' website to help you if you have a small audience to begin with. Let's assume you have 1,000 visitors to your website every month. Not brand new, but not much activity. If you go to a publication that receives 50,000 visitors each month and offer quality content to them, there is an opportunity to open you to a much wider audience. Online publications typically welcome fresh content. Furthermore, this may provide you with SEO benefits.

What can be even more beneficial is what I refer to as "climbing the ladder." After you contribute to your first publication, you can reference that article in future outreach. This adds credibility that you will deliver quality content and have been vetted by others in the past. For each contribution, you should reach higher than before. If your first contribution was to a website with 10,000 monthly visitors, aim for a site that reaches 50,000 monthly visitors. From there, reach out to sites with 500,000 visitors, and so on. This is how you can reach major publishers, building credibility, and gaining those *"As featured in . . ."* badges of honor.

Audio content is steadily growing in popularity due to podcasting becoming a force in media and entertainment. As larger publications and individual entertainers have taken strongholds in podcasting, the consumer markets are becoming savvier in how to find, subscribe, and listen in.

Make note how consumer behavior changes in the general public. People love the on-demand nature of podcasts, in similar fashion to how behaviors and expectations are changing Hollywood. With the availability of on-demand streaming options, the television industry is shaken and movie watching disrupted. The largest media companies today are those who capitalized on this change in consumer behavior.

Podcast growth is aligning with this change. They may be viewed as an ongoing effort or seasonally. They may be guest-driven or monologues and dialogues by the host(s). There are numerous formats that can work well. Most important is this: you begin with a format and commit to the ongoing creation for that first season or an initial stretch of creation time.

Podcasts fail when they are given up on before they gain traction, leaving them underpromoted and underutilized. Stay committed to the ongoing development, and you can establish a unique channel to reach new audiences and deepen connection with existing followers. Today, you arrive at podcasting at a prime point of the trend as the market becomes more sophisticated.

Video content and video marketing provides depth to interactions due to the nature of video: you *hear* someone's voice and you *see* them (or supporting visuals). This is an excellent way to increase intimacy over written mediums, while having a sound technical basis for search engine rankings and creative distribution. In addition, we can see social networks such as Instagram, Facebook, and Snapchat becoming more video-centric. These networks are growing distribution platforms.

How do you select between the different forms? Offering variety helps to align your content to people who are predisposed to consuming content through auditory, visual, or written means.

Also consider your brand, competition, and market. Is the industry stale and corporate-feeling? Can you add a touch of personality and intimacy through a specific channel, perhaps having a designated "spokesperson" who writes engaging content, records entertaining podcasts, and films educational video? Focusing on relationship development at scale is the mindset you need when approaching content creation.

> **Guiding Principle:** Content marketing is an all-encompassing term for any materials you create for your audience that *pulls* them to you. This includes written, audio, and video form. Content should always be at least one thing: educational, engaging, or entertaining.

Social Media Marketing

My philosophy on social media marketing has not changed over the last five years. General rule of thumb for a small business: post at least weekly so people who do search for you know you are actively in business, but do not rely on it as a revenue source to your business. Though exceptions exist, financial ROI can be challenging with social. That does *not* mean you should disregard it!

While suggesting a lack of ROI may be harsh, and it will upset the professional social media marketers reading this, this viewpoint changes when introducing social advertising, networks that do no throttle reach based on payment, and specific circumstances. Consider a channel like Facebook. If you rely on posting to your Facebook Page to grow your business, you will surely suffer, as without paying Facebook for increased exposure, you reach a minuscule segment of your following. If you do pay, you unlock powerful opportunities, which we will explore in the social advertising section.

If you lack an advertising budget, focus on unthrottled platforms relevant to your market, such as Instagram (2018). Now, social media marketing becomes useful. Compound the lack of "pay to play" with potential exposure from proper hashtag use, engagement, and influencer integration, and you have a meaningful social media presence.

Having talent that can design and execute an Instagram strategy is necessary, though, unless it all made sense when I mentioned *hashtags, engagement,* and *influencers.* (Influencer marketing requires payment, so this will be found in the Paid Advertising section of this chapter.) This is one example to illustrate the thinking.

For larger organizations, the dependence on their marketing to be on lead generation lessens, and social media becomes a more apt channel for content distribution, community engagement, and customer service. At scale, social media should be a primary channel to share content your company creates, as well as curation of relevant information to your audience that can be found from other entities. The focus, again, is on deepening relationships by being valuable to your market: educate, engage, entertain.

For community engagement, you can leverage social media to pose questions, drive discussion, and hold giveaways and contests. Again, we want people to feel relevance and personality in their interactions with your company, and these tactics can help to accomplish that.

Customer service is a major concern, operation, expense, and opportunity for larger corporations. Social media is where people congregate, particularly as people across generations become more accustomed to using social media and mobile devices than visiting stores, waiting in lines, and making phone calls. The immediacy of response outpaces email support, as well, furthering preference social media as a customer service channel to some markets.

As with content creation, offer a variety of options to align your servicing with your customers' preferences. It should be as simple and enjoyable for them to contact you as possible, right? So, look to social media as an outlet. For example, many large corporations have teams dedicated on Twitter to handle customer service issues – which is helpful across channels for positive public relations or avoiding PR disasters.

> **Guiding Principle:** Social media is typically *not* a source for lead generation or sales. It should not be neglected, however. If you have talent to execute on channels that fit your audience, there is potential value. In larger organizations, social media is becoming a leading channel for customer service and community building.

Community Development

Communities drive connection, loyalty, and appreciation. As a community grows, the network effect should become stronger, creating a compounding and mutual value for company and customers alike.

Network effect is a concept of a product or service gaining additional value as more people use it. This is experienced in many of the world's strongest businesses. With Google, as more people search, more companies create higher quality content, which provides a better experience for searchers and a higher ranking on Google's search results page for the company.

We see this with Amazon's marketplace, too. As more buyers visit Amazon, the standards for the products and customer service of vendors raises, resulting in a better experience for buyers, as well as more buyers gravitating to Amazon for the sellers' benefit.

The same is true of online communities. As more people join, there should be greater benefits by more valuable information shared, speedier responses, increased breadth of perspective, and stronger attendance for community events, virtual or in-person.

Creating a community online can be a private offering to customers or open publicly. It can be housed on your own website or provided through an existing platform such as Facebook Groups or a dedicated subreddit on Reddit.com. How do you make these decisions?

Start with what would provide maximal value to members of the community. What would make them stay and return again and again? What does scaling community membership look like in six months, in a year, and in three years? Where is our market most comfortable? Are there any benefits of using our own platform compared to an existing, out-of-the-box platform?

> **Guiding Principle:** Communities help you to stay connected to customers while they connect with each other. There is a network effect as the community scales. Nonetheless, it has to be valuable, simple to be actively engaged in, and fitting to your audience.

Database & Email Marketing

Database marketing is the building of lists of prospects and customers, and the outreach to them. Typically, in the digital world, this focuses on the use of email marketing, though there can be further uses of databases that extend into paid advertising.

Email remains the most reliable way to cost-effectively reach people who have previously agreed to being contacted by you. While there are benefits of other channels, such as text message marketing or direct mail, email is where I recommend most companies to begin their efforts until communications here are systemized.

Email comes in three formats: newsletters (consistent), special broadcasts (ad hoc), and autoresponders (automated sequences).

Salience is one of the most important outcomes of marketing. Being "top of mind" should be addressed in your marketing strategies. With email as a mechanism to reach that presence, the consistency of a newsletter makes this a core element of the system, not an aspiration.

Newsletters are a channel for content distribution. Follow the rule of being educational, engaging, and entertaining. Frequency depends on your market and resources. Once a week to once a month is sufficient. More frequent can be risky, unless offering a "daily deals" newsletter *and* having proper resources to execute. Less than monthly leaves you too out-of-touch with your audience. Always opt to start more conservatively to gauge your resource needs to execute this.

Special broadcasts are created on an ad hoc basis. These are relevant during holidays, cultural events, or new business or product developments and news. Careful use can provide excellent exposure in a cost-efficient manner.

While they can be helpful as part of specific campaigns, your focus should always be to first develop a meaningful newsletter as that provides the structure to make email a place where your database members are willing, open, and eager to see your communications.

Autoresponders are automated email sequences that are dripped out based on someone taking a specific action. There are countless uses of these, but here's how to think of them: they become your salesperson in virtual form, providing the right information at the right time in the right sequence so that the viewer will be better informed and capable of making decisions to move forward.

Visualize what your sales process looks like from when someone first calls in or visits your store to when they make a purchase. The conversations that take place and the information that is shared in this process can be digitized into email format, where you can leverage written word, audio, and video. The conversations are broken into segments and distributed in an automated sequence. It does the work of the salesperson without any individual time put forth for that individual prospect.

While I do not view autoresponders as a way to replace salespeople, it can supplement their efforts. While people are not always apt to respond to sales calls, meetings, and visits, they can open their email at their own leisure and where they feel safe. Let the email provide the supplemental educating, engaging, and entertaining when the sales teams can't.

> **Guiding Principle:** There are three forms of email communications: newsletters, special broadcasts, and autoresponders. Use all three strategically for a consistent and meaningful connection to your audience.

Search Engine Optimization (SEO)

SEO is housed under content marketing because I believe it should be focused on *quality content creation* and search engine friendly website structure. The methodologies of SEO that were focused on filling articles with keywords and running them through artificial networks continues to die as it is replaced by the authenticity of quality content offered on trusted sites.

This results in a dependency on creating content for your own website and contributing to other websites that point back to your company's site as the source. To rank your website well, consider two questions in contributing content: how many websites do I need pointing to my site, and what are the high authority sites that search engines respect in my market?

Speaking to the former on quantity of websites pointing to yours, you can measure and compare the number of references you receive in comparison to key competitors. This is something any SEO researcher can handle for you. It provides a benchmark. A savvy SEO expert can help you determine how to compete over time based on competition and the market.

On the latter point related to quality, different websites have more authority with search engines than others.

There are a number of factors at play here, but it can be quite obvious that Google places greater trust in a major news publication with millions of monthly visits than an independent website with a thousand monthly visitors. Your goal is to simply "climb the ladder" and continue contributing to larger market-relevant publications that have greater followings and greater authority with search engines.

Create content to host on your own website, as well, and ensure that it is properly structured for user experience and for search engines to understand what the content is about. Creating your own content is a way to fuel your SEO, resulting in higher rankings for relevant searches. Distribute your efforts between self-hosted content and contributions.

SEO also involves proper, consistent listings on directories across the web. These "citations" often report your company name, address, and phone number, along with a company description or background. This includes sites like Google, Bing, Yahoo, YP, Superpages, Yelp, and social media sites. This is particularly helpful with businesses that serve a local area ("Local SEO"). This will be less relevant for large organizations to address.

The above points touch on major *off-site SEO* concepts to address. In addition to this, *on-site SEO* must be properly handled so that you are building your efforts on a strong foundation. On-site SEO can be technical in nature, involving the website's structure and speed. It also relates to proper user experience, with simple navigation and helpful resources. Again, content creation on your own website is important.

As always, refer to the research you conducted in Phase 1 to understand how to structure your SEO properly, based on what your market is interested in and what they search for in their buying process. Build a strong foundation by developing your on-site SEO, and then carry forth efforts to enhance off-site SEO with proper citations being built. This is your low-hanging fruit.

Creating content for your site requires resources of time, talent, and treasure, while contributing takes additional resources to build connections and relationships to other publications. I recommend these efforts come after on-site and initial citation building. Once that foundation is prepared, this may become a primary source of activity for your business.

> **Guiding Principle:** SEO plays an important role in your presence online and requires proper attention and investment. Focus on building your foundation first with on-site SEO; then progress to off-site SEO through content creation and contributing.

2.2.2
Push: Paid Advertising

Paid advertising is a "push" strategy. That means you are not waiting for prospects to find you. Instead, you are *pushing* your message in front of them. Fortunately, we can do this with more relevance than ever conceivable in decades past. While advertising may hold a negative connotation, you can develop campaigns that people *want* to receive.

Search Advertising

Search advertising primarily refers to *Google Ads* (previously called *Google AdWords*). This is how companies advertise on Google when someone searches a relevant query, presenting their websites above those in the organic listings. Other terms marketers use for this are pay-per-click or PPC advertising, paid search, and search engine marketing.

Google is the primary player in this market, accounting for close to 80% of all search advertising revenue in the United States. The remaining 20% is primarily split among Microsoft (Bing), Yahoo, Yelp, Amazon, Ask, and AOL (Verizon).

It is difficult to predict which channels are perfect for you, but here's what we do know: Google is a dominant force for a reason and experiences the greatest volume of general search engine traffic. Bing, in my experience, has unpredictable results, occasionally resulting in higher quality traffic, though often at a premium.

Meanwhile, Amazon's advertising services can be helpful for product companies, particularly as the tentacles of Amazon spreads across physical stores (e.g., *Whole Foods*) and the Internet of Things (e.g., *Alexa*).

Research and be skeptical of every platform. For example, Yelp appears like a perfect platform for local business, and their sales teams are committed to convincing you of such. However, I have only witnessed negative experiences and poor business practices with the company firsthand, and there are thousands of accounts to corroborate such.

In search advertising, remember that people are actively seeking something specific, whether a solution to a specific problem, an actual product, or a specific company. You can target accordingly, but also ensure that your advert and the unique web page it sends people to *("landing page")* are aligned to the experience. It should make logical sense and move people towards making a decision in working with you. That initial micro-commitment must progress the relationship forward, whether that be a purchase or otherwise.

The buyer's journey involves going through stages of initial awareness, consideration of one's options, and decisions on a specific solution. Typically, search advertisers are closer to the decision stage as the searcher is actively seeking a solution, but always align according to a specific moment in the buying process.

> **Guiding Principle:** Search advertising presents your company on search engine results pages for relevant queries by the user. Align your company and messaging to relevant queries according to the buyer's journey to have a powerful marketing mechanism in place.

Social Advertising

Social media has taken the forefront of marketing in recent years. As you may have guessed from my previously shared viewpoint of social media marketing as a channel, I don't find it deserving of such praise if your goal is business growth. Social media has a fit, but for sales-oriented organizations, its potential is limiting and the real opportunity is deceiving.

Yet, I believe social advertising is an untapped, underutilized, and misunderstood goldmine:

- It allows us to leverage Big Data, even for small business
- It enables data-centric results, so we can use hard metrics to define success
- It provides an opportunity to *"fish where the fish are swimming,"* meaning we are approaching potential customers where they are comfortable and congregating willingly and independently

Social advertising channels include popular platforms like Facebook, Instagram, Twitter, Pinterest, YouTube, LinkedIn, and Snapchat. Facebook pioneered social advertising due to their integration of their own comprehensive data with numerous Big Data providers, such as Oracle, Mastercard, Epsilon, BlueKai, Nielsen, Datalogix, Acxiom, and Experian. As we witnessed in 2018 when Facebook faced pushback from the public and congress, things can change dramatically in digital marketing, so we always need our finger on the pulse.

LinkedIn provides a professional atmosphere and career-related targeting. Snapchat has a deep personal-focus as part of the platform, and therefore provides a more intimate connection point. No single platform is superior, but each provides benefits to different businesses, situations, and needs.

In deciding on advertising channels to pursue, consider as criteria:

- The data and targeting options available
- Where your consumers are most comfortable online

- Which platforms your consumers have a higher propensity to visit
- Where you can garner adequate trust

> **Guiding Principle:** Social advertising is powerful due to the environment that ads are presented in and the data available to us as marketers. It is separate from social media marketing, but can work in conjunction with it. Selecting the right channels for your audience is paramount.

Niche Advertising

Advertising is not limited to search and social, though those are often the go-to channels based on dependability and familiarity.

However, niche communities may have their own advertising and sponsorship opportunities that provide a unique audience at affordable rates. You can typically reach these *communities* through message boards and publication newsletters.

Another benefit is aligning to the culture of that community. For example, Reddit is a social news aggregator and discussion website and is the fourth most visited website in the United States and the eight most visited in the world (2018). Within Reddit exists over a million subreddits focused on specific areas of interest *(niches)*. You can target advertisements based on topics people are interested in or even specific subreddits they engage with.

Online publications often have sponsoring opportunities, where you may participate in webinars, advertise in newsletters, or be shared in social media channels. Again, the specificity of the audience and the costs need to be considered.

> **Guiding Principle:** Niche advertising may be an economical way to deliver a highly targeted message to a specific audience. Sponsorships may also be considered if the placement and positioning is beneficial to you, as well as the results trackable.

Retargeting

If you have ever noticed an ad for something you were looking at previously following you around the web for days, weeks, or months at a time, this is retargeting at work. You have been identified as a potential customer based on your engagement with a certain web page, and now these ads are presented to you in hopes that you will return and purchase.

Retargeting is driven on the principle of being salient. Knowing you will buy when the time is right for you, retargeting presents the option to buy (or deepen the relationship in some manner) at various times after you have engaged, hoping to find the right time in your Buyer's Journey.

This can be platform-specific, such as Facebook Advertising's retargeting or Google's "remarketing." However, there are also independent retargeting platforms that can connect to your website and present ads back to people who previously visited.

If you understand this concept, visualize it as part of your marketing flow. At what stages is it relevant to get information back in front of a potential customer? Perhaps on a page describing a specific product or service, what it is like to work with your company, on pricing information, or the "contact us" page.

Seek out key areas where people could have made a decision to step forward, yet didn't. Using retargeting, you can present that next step to them again so that when they are ready, it is easily available.

> **Guiding Principle:** Retargeting is a powerful way to stay salient in the mind of the consumer who previously engaged with your business, presenting a next step in the nurturing and sales process for them to re-engage with your company.

Influencer Marketing

Influencer marketing remains an untapped goldmine. While it is a popular topic, the execution of a well-thought out influencer campaign and how that operates is rarely performed and perfected. Instead, we see "PR spikes" of an influencer being involved periodically, but lack a systematic integration.

Influencer marketing works similarly to celebrity endorsements. You are hiring someone with a loyal following to endorse your company, products or services. On a small scale, influencers will agree to these arrangements in exchange for free products or services. At a larger scale, influencers typically require payment for their endorsement. As this form of marketing matures, payment will be a standard even among smaller influencers and individual endorsements will increase in investment.

Make influencer marketing a core element of your strategy today if it fits your business and market. You may tap into an asset that fuels your business in a creative and prosperous manner. There's great opportunity for this early-stage marketing activity.

> **Guiding Principle:** Influencer marketing is akin to celebrity endorsements of the modern age. In this case, "celebrity" can be anyone with a loyal online audience, whether the influencer has 100,000 or millions of followers.

Follow Advertising Best Practices

Ultimately, tracking is the most important element of all marketing. This is particularly true with advertising because these "push" channels should have a direct and clear correlation between investment and outcome.

If you cannot track it, do not do it. Fortunately, this is not of great concern when it comes to major channels, such as those provided by Google, Microsoft, and Amazon. It may be a concern for smaller publications that provide advertising and sponsorship if they lack infrastructure to prove results. Nonetheless, you can often create a separate environment for those channels to isolate relevant metrics and handle tracking entirely on your own, and while not as simple, it is sufficient in most instances.

Immediacy of results should not be over-prioritized. Commit to a channel for at least six months before you dismiss it. The first three months are when 80% of your optimization is handled, resulting in a stronger campaign beyond that period. After six months, you may start seeing results from leads generated in the first month. The campaign begins to compound on itself, meaning even if all metrics remain the same three months later, results improve because of the ongoing awareness and intrigue building element.

Remember that sales come from two things: trust and timing. Even if we do all we can to develop trust, the timing has to be right, and so, return on investment is best determined at minimum six months from launch.

Assuming proper tracking is in place and you are prepared to commit to a strategy, a scientific approach to testing is the next priority. This means taking one variable at a time, testing it to a point of statistical significance, digesting and translating those results, and forming a new hypothesis to test.

The actual scientific method should be used as an ongoing process in your marketing. You start with a hypothesis you want to test based on the available data. You create a test that will provide the answer to this hypothesis. You run the test to generate data. You review this data, making observations of trends and results. You form a new hypothesis and begin the process again.

How do you determine the hypothesis? Focus on high-leverage tests you can conduct. Major strategic elements of campaigns include the audiences, the demographics, the messaging, and the key visuals. Tactical elements that can be tested, but provide lower returns for the tests include things like page layout, testimonials used, and button colors. These play a role, but do not alter results as greatly.

Furthermore, if you test tactical elements while targeting the wrong people with the wrong message, you may optimize for the wrong people. In the very least, you will gain little while spending more than necessary on an unoptimized audience and message.

How do you ensure statistical significance? You need to allow your tests to run to a point where there are undeniable results based on statistical variation. This requires consideration of *data hygiene,* as well. For example, one common issue is time. If you run a test for just a few days, there is concern that the days of the week influenced the results, whether skewing performance positively or negatively. Testing for at least a week spreads results over a time period that can be properly compared in future tests and lessens time-related distortions. This is how you can address variances and keep test data clean.

> **Guiding Principle:** For all advertising, follow simple guidelines: tracking of sales-oriented metrics is vital; avoid over-prioritizing immediacy of results; and approach testing variables scientifically.

PHASE 2 CONCLUSION

Strategy development is complete when you have ensured the following was reviewed and analyzed:

Reviewed Processes & Technology

- Online value proposition
- Digital touchpoints
- Digital marketing funnels
- Customer experience innovations
- Customer loyalty programming
- Marketing technology – "MarTech"
- Evaluating your website as your central hub

In this section, you need to give reasonable thought to each area and conduct appropriate exercises. This will take you some time with exploration of each topic, forming discussions, and finalizing decisions on what to engage further.

For example, you may decide to forgo any customer loyalty programming at this time. However, you may find areas of improvement needed through your digital touchpoints exercise. You can now identify those areas of improvement needed and design an action plan to address each during the next phase.

Selected Communication Channels

- Pull: content marketing
- Push: paid advertising

In this section, you were provided a basic overview of each channel at an executive level, with the most salient points of each addressed. You should review these channels as philosophies in approach to the market and value to the business. You should be able to identify what channels are relevant and why, based on a high-level strategic perspective.

Going forward, as we define budget and resources, you can begin to identify what channels to prioritize and projects to deploy as we explore Phase 3: Guided Implementation.

PHASE 3
GUIDED IMPLEMENTATION

At this point, we have collected and conducted comprehensive research, defined what processes and technology will support us, and decided upon proper channels to reach our consumers based on our study of the market and competition. Now, we need to take actionable steps to implementing the plan.

I love the classic framework of "People, Process, Product." I believe all three require adequate attention for a healthy business and at least one should be exceptional for a business to succeed.

For implementation, we will focus on *People,* "The Execution Team", and *Process*, the "Management Protocols". Our one assumption in this section: your *Product* is strong, including if there is digitization of it as part of this strategy, and that you have or can gain *People* to assist you in digitizing it and executing it in its new form.

Before going further, please review all of your activities from Phase 2. Since each reader will have his or her own outcomes, I cannot walk you through your individual scenario of how to execute accordingly in this section. However, as we outline the people and processes involved, you will be able to align each to your Phase 2 findings. (For example, you will have a set of channels selected and will make sure you acquire the talent to execute on those channels.)

3.1
IDENTIFY THE EXECUTION TEAM

Your execution team may include your existing staff, new employees, or external partners such as consultants, freelancers, and agencies. Finding the right mix depends upon resources, competencies, and longevity of need for the given projects.

3.1.1
Agile Marketing Methodology

You may or may not have heard of the term "agile marketing" before. This methodology emerged from the world of project management, specifically for software development. Then, it spread to other disciplines, including marketing.

Agile marketing is simply a philosophy. This philosophy emphasizes the importance of identifying key project segments, breaking them into short phases of work, and dividing tasks out from within each phase. As you progress through each phase, you rapidly run an experiment, pause, review findings, and repeat the process.

You constantly run micro-tests, hitting checkpoints as you go, rather than running and testing separate full-scale campaigns and only finding out if they are worthwhile or not after a large expenditure of time and money.

While agile may simply be a philosophy, it isn't simple. Success is reliant on the people, processes, and technology involved in each situation. Although everyone would like marketing initiatives developed in days, rather than weeks or months, you still need to manage various moving parts.

Today's consumers are conditioned to be impatient and to value relevance. That is the premise successful social networks and websites are designed within. Taking longer than 2-3 seconds to load? Skip. Something new happening in the world? Let's check it out! And so, agility with your marketing is important.

This manifests through your ability to take data, analytics, and an understanding of your consumer base and use that information to design communications that matter to them – quickly.

A small business may test one element at any given time. A large enterprise may scale their testing to run dozens or hundreds of tests simultaneously each week. But tests are determined by statistical significance and require proper budget to find such. So regardless of scale of operation, you should focus on quality testing procedures.

The Process

Agile marketing is not simply about quickly testing, learning from those tests, and retesting. The agile marketing philosophy also incorporates cross-functional involvement. That means HR, legal teams, IT, finance, and other related departments must be involved. Why? There can be no agile marketing if there are bottlenecks due to legal reviews, budgets being released, or any other potential risk.

Agile marketing needs to be adopted by all parties involved, which extends beyond internal employees. External teams must also contribute to this methodology, which may prove more challenging due to the disconnect between your external partners and internal team. This includes partnering agencies and technology vendors.

For agile marketing to become part of your organization, you are going to need to prepare in a few ways. First, you need a clear vision as to *why* this method of operation makes sense. If you are asking people to change how they behave, you need a compelling reason, and removing as much uncertainty about the process is helpful.

To set a clear vision for this, first clarify *why*. You may identify a certain customer segment that you want to improve acquisition among or a segment that you would like to see return for additional business. For example, you may say, "we want to attract more small business banking customers who are at the start of their new ventures," or, "we want to make the referral generating process more effective for our new homeowner mortgage clients," or, "we want to effectively provide cross-sell opportunities to our ecommerce customers in a way that they will be enthusiastic about."

It will also be important to make sure you have proper marketing technology in place, so be sure to review this thoroughly. (This is covered in the MarTech section of the book.)

In addition to vision, you must provide proper support from the leadership to everyone involved in the project. Leadership's championing the project includes support being communicated, adequate funding provided, and autonomy given with project responsibility to the executing parties.

Building a strong core team that will adopt and apply the agile philosophy is vital. This team can work at high speed if you ensure you remove roadblocks and provide adequate support. They may also, however, require freedom from their typical job duties. This may be a part-time activity or a full-time activity, as fit for your individual case.

The team will coalesce into a project group, sometimes referred to as a "squad," "crew," "war room," or "tribe." You can toss any name on it, so long as it doesn't appear to limit the group to certain departments.

A typical agile squad would include a core team of project managers, strategists, copywriters, creative directors, designers, developers, analytics leads, and relevant channel experts (social media, Facebook Advertising, Google Ads, etc). The total size of the group should not exceed twelve, as groups tend to get slowed down at that size.

In addition to this, the extended agile squad would include a team of associated parties, such as IT, legal, and finance. *Who* precisely is involved will depend upon what type of project you are working on and what skills are needed.

It is important that squads have clear lines of communication with each other in the group, as well as any outside parties that will be contacted in the process. Speedy communication allows for speedy action. Consider internal communication tools, chat systems, and project management technology.

Aside from the logistics of communication, agreements must be clearly established as to how quickly communications are to be had and decisions to be made. This is particularly relevant with legal, IT, and finance contact involvement.

In each meeting, which may be once or twice each week, a group leader will set the agenda, establish priorities, define what is to be tested, manage the backlog of ideas, inspire the generation of new ideas, facilitate discussion on existing tests, manage resources, and plan for the upcoming "sprint" (a 1-2 week work cycle).

As for leadership, they again champion the project, but will be passively involved. Regular meetings should share with leadership what has been tested, accomplished, and what lies ahead in an "executive summary" format with select key metrics made salient for brevity and transparency. This meeting should be no more frequent than monthly.

To summarize, here is how your agile marketing team is developed in three steps:

First, you are going to establish your reason for forming this team. What will it help you accomplish? This will help you to identify the core and external team members required to make this a success.

Second, you will begin facilitating meetings once or twice a week where ideas will be generated, tested, and reviewed. Create a hypothesis, set KPIs (Key Performance Indicators) to meet, and run the test. Prioritize ideas based on ease of implementation and likely magnitude of impact.

Third, you will manage the projects between meetings, ensuring that initiatives are successfully launched and bottlenecks are alleviated. Remember, tests are typically run in a one- or two-week cycle, or "sprint."

If you are in a large organization, a single team of around ten people may not suffice for the amount of testing you want to accomplish. If this is the case, I would urge you to first start and manage this first team for at least two months. This provides you with great education on the process, as well as proper focus to make sure this team is running effectively and efficiently.

> **Guiding Principle:** Take the agile marketing philosophy as an approach for your marketing going forward. It allows rapid testing and reduces waste (time, money). Ultimately, this process can spread across your marketing department and organization at large, but you must follow a process to ensure success.

3.1.2
In-House & Outsourcing

For smaller companies, I typically recommend a mixed approach: an internal asset who understands marketing best practices, but external partners who "get their hands dirty" and handle execution.

This internal asset is who should be able to determine whether an external partner or internal new hire meets a competency, is a fit, and has relevant expertise and skills for the given assignment. That means the internal asset must stay abreast of what truly works and what is a fad, what best practices are, and most of all, they need to understand the types of strategic philosophies I am sharing throughout this book.

In-house staff to handle all marketing activities typically does not work unless you operate a mid-sized company. Smaller companies cannot afford to hire specialized talent to maintain a high-quality level and therefore sacrifice quality when a few people handle *all* marketing activities (or worse, one person).

The growth of the marketing team should be organic as specialized skill sets become needed on a full-time basis.

I recommend you begin hiring when it appears that an in-house staff member would have 25 hours of work a week to handle. Chances are it could take a bit longer, and the role should have some buffer time for growth, meetings, and additional needs.

Whether you are hiring in-house or an external partner, you need to validate the prospective execution team members. With external partners, the two factors that are most prominent in my experience are *communication* and *expertise*.

It is common to find someone who communicates clearly and quickly, but is not particularly great at what they do. Likewise, there are many true experts at their craft that cannot articulate what they do and why or simply disappear for far too long. Find someone who is talented in communication and their domain, and you have someone to add to your shortlist.

Beyond this, there is great debate between depth of experience and breadth of experience. This can relate to the industries one has worked with or the tasks performed, such as advertising on a specific channel. Generally, I recommend finding someone who has depth of experience on one channel. Remember, we are growing the marketing team organically as our demands on specific channels provide sufficient workload for a specialized individual to handle. Accordingly, talent in specific areas is prioritized as a baseline. Further, channels operate in unique ways and change often, requiring consistent attention and development.

If that is our baseline, how do we handle the depth versus breadth of expertise debate related to the industry? It would make sense that someone who intimately knows your industry would be more fitting for the role. However, if you are not in a highly-specialized field and industry regulations, history, and jargon would not be a significant factor in training, then opt for someone with breadth of expertise across industries. Often, the best ideas and lessons originate from what is being done across industries, rather than what is typical of one industry.

When it comes to external partners, consultants are helpful in providing strategic insight for specific developments. Freelancers provide affordability to your execution efforts.

Agencies provide security in having a breadth of specialists in their company or network (at least the agencies you choose *should* have dedicated specialists and not marketing generalists). Agencies may be more expensive than freelancers, but provide benefits of someone else hiring and managing the individuals who do the work and ensuring they are aligned in the projects they undergo. Think of agencies as small collections of freelancers, typically led or supplemented by a consultant providing strategic insight. Again, not typical of all agencies, but this should be what you look for.

Regardless of whether you are hiring an internal employee or external partner, take careful consideration to *who* you employ. Digital is a field that requires specialized focus for exceptional results, so opt for specialists over generalists. You want people who will take action and provide insight to you, not simply follow guidelines given to them ("order takers").

I have found the best way to evaluate talent, particularly in digital, is to run a "split test" on the talent. If you can shortlist two or three candidates, provide each of them with a small, finite project they can deliver to you. This should be a paid assignment. Channel strategies tend to work well here, if relevant to the role to be fulfilled. Provide the same instructions to each, but allow them to complete it as they wish. The right candidate will ask you the right set of questions and provide you with an insightful deliverable.

Certainly, you will want to give consideration to factors such as cultural fit, but this test project will help you experience that firsthand, along with communication proficiency and true expertise. A small additional investment upfront will pay off in the short and long-term many times over. Having the right people is exceptionally important.

> **Guiding Principle:** Hire an internal asset that deeply understands digital. They act as your strategist and verify legitimacy, need, and fit of new hires or external partners. Prioritize specialists over generalists. Determine fit based on two factors: communication proficiency and subject-matter expertise. Finally, whether a prospective internal hire or external partner, split test their performance before fully committing.

3.1.3
Restructuring Your Marketing Department

A painful truth you must face is that today's marketing team may not be tomorrow's. When you are redeveloping your firm to operate in a digital era, your people must evolve with it. There is great value in many in-house personnel, which is why training, coaching, and advising is important to bolster those individuals.

The restructuring of your department depends upon your digital strategy: the communication channels and supporting technologies and processes. This dictates what needs to be done and who is needed for it. From there are the decisions of what is done in-house, based on project demands, skills and resources, and what is outsourced. From this exercise, you will define a hierarchy in the marketing department, starting with someone to lead all efforts.

Under the marketing leadership, you can begin development of two divisions: the content marketing (pull) division and the advertising (push) division. The marketing executive should have no more than ten direct reports at any time between these two divisions. Likewise, if one division reaches seven direct reports, it is likely that the next hire should be someone to manage those individuals.

For example, if there are seven in the content marketing division and two in the advertising division, it will likely be better for the organization to find a leader of content marketing than to further invest in another advertising team member and leaving the full ten reports to the lone marketing executive.

Ultimately, you may find some individuals had jobs that no longer exist, and there may not be a new job fitting for them. You may be able to supplement a gap with advisory, training, or coaching for that individual.

Nevertheless, while few of us can find contentedness in firing, there are times when letting someone go is the most logical move for the company. And if it is the right move for the company, it will be the right move for that individual.

> **Guiding Principle:** Restructuring relies on your needs based on your new digital strategy. With communication channels, technology, and processes changing, the department must evolve, as well. You may consider designing the department to operate in channel divisions: content marketing and advertising.

3.1.4
Budget Reallocation

Allocating budgets between traditional and digital is an ever-moving target. This makes sense, as the capabilities of and understanding of digital continue to evolve and has remained in its infancy for quite a while. However, it appears that small and large companies are universally realizing opportunities online and shifting budgets accordingly.

If you need to develop a marketing budget, a simple approach is to take 5–10% of your annual revenue and designate that amount for the budget. This is a common practice. The range may be narrowed by company type, as B2B tends to stay around 5–7% and B2C tends to stay around 7–10%. Also, aggressiveness based on objectives and available funds may increase budgets. Smaller companies may seek to invest up to 15% of their revenues, if possible. Note, these figures may not include salaries and overhead, so this should be taken into account as you finalize your budget.

Within your set marketing budget, most companies should dedicate 30-40% of the budget to digital, mobile, and social. A more modest, "toe in the water" approach would be 20-30% of your budget. If you wish to invest less than that, the assumption would be you are in special market circumstances or are not serious about or confident in your investment.

For more serious players in the digital space, or companies that operate primarily online, an increased investment is acceptable if you can show a return on investment for the year. Many traditional companies are investing 40-50%, while online businesses invest 90-100% of their budget on digital.

We are simply trying to follow consumer trends – or even predict them when possible. As we see more consumers increasing fluency with digital, mobile, and social, and we see the greater propensity to go online than visit a store or call in, we need our marketing to meet this new standard. Consumer behavior is different today; allow your marketing budgets to be, as well.

> **Guiding Principle:** Digital requires an investment, and this dictates the way you approach execution of your strategy. There are simple ways to determine this based on your existing marketing budget or revenue. A portion of this budget must be dedicated to digital activities.

3.2
ESTABLISH MANAGEMENT PROTOCOLS

The management protocols that dictate how your business operates, are what allow for innovations, quality improvements, and cost-efficiencies. The protocols related to digital we will focus on now are what enables you to effectively manage your new marketing efforts.

These protocols can be applied to any online or offline marketing, as well as across other impact areas, such as customer service, sales, human resources, accounting, and so on. This is another reason we emphasize principles and philosophies, rather than tactics.

3.2.1
Measurement, KPI Tracking & Campaign Optimizations

We previously discussed the importance of tracking and proper testing protocols so that we are certain our efforts are effective and improving. In that, we mentioned the importance of statistical significance and the "scientific method" approach. We will now look at measurement at a high-level view for a marketing leader.

Attribution of Results

One consideration of measurement is how attribution is handled. There are two forms of single attribution: first touch and last touch. This means that if a sale is made, it attributes the conversion *entirely* to either the first point of contact with the buyer *or* the last point of contact with the buyer. The designated channel receives the attribution and this is calculated in the return on investment (ROI). Single attribution is the least accurate, but easiest and least costly to implement.

To enhance single attribution, you can account for Revenue Cycle Projections, if possible. With this focus, you are not relying solely on the basic data given. You use your historical data to predict the true value of the leads and sales generated. This requires insight on conversion rates and customer lifetime value, but can help you realize the true value of activities with long-term perspective, rather than immediate results alone. Remember, marketing should be viewed as a process spanning many months before determining what the true results are. With this data, you will extrapolate initial results based on the historical trends to determine the actual returns you *will* realize.

Multi-touch attribution is more accurate, but more complex and costly to implement. Nonetheless, if you are capable of setting this up, the added insights likely outweigh the additional costs. In this model, you may attribute sales by distributing percentages of that sale to different programs according to the recency or the significance of the touch. This allows fairer distribution of ROI as it is not typical that a single channel accounted for *all* influence and results.

The most complex, insightful, and costly is a full Market Mix Modeling approach. In this regard, you take into account all marketing programs, as you do with multi-touch attribution, but also incorporate internal and external factors. Internal factors may relate to the price, product, promotion, and place. External factors may relate to the economy, competition, and consumer behavior. This is not typically relevant for small or mid-sized companies, unless a healthy amount of data and resources are available, such as in the finance sector.

Implementing an attribution model requires decisioning and protocols. This can be established for the comprehensive marketing initiative (results from the overall marketing budget), as well as individual marketing activities (results from a channel-specific advertising campaign).

For the marketing initiative as a whole, let us assume you have an annual marketing budget of $1,000,000 and allocated 35% to digital activities, or $350,000. You must determine metrics that will indicate whether you have experienced a return on that $350,000 investment.

The measurements we use should connect the marketing investment back to the revenue generated, while also accounting for sales investments and influences, where possible.

Customer Acquisition Cost

First, let's look at the Customer Acquisition Cost (CAC). You may think of this as the cost per new sale. You need to take into account all marketing and sales costs, including programs, advertising, salaries, commissions, bonuses, and overhead relative to the time period. Then, to find the CAC, use the following equation:

$$\frac{\text{Marketing \& Sales Costs}}{\text{Total New Customers}} = \text{Customer Acquisition Cost}$$

For example, let's say your costs are $950,000 for the year and you gained 2,000 new customers. That means the equation is ($950,000 ÷ 2,000) = $475 Customer Acquisition Cost. If your CAC is $475 and your revenue from the initial sale is $1,000 with a 50% profit margin, you know that earning $2M in revenue and $1M in profit makes this profitable. However, you may also wish to see greater profit, which may require increasing lifetime value beyond the initial sale or optimizing for this initial sale to reduce CAC. However, you do not know where you stand until you determine the Customer Acquisition Cost.

Marketing's Contribution to Sales

Let's consider how marketing has contributed to the new customer while removing the sales function. The equation is as follows:

$$\frac{\text{Total Marketing Costs}}{\text{Total Marketing + Sales Costs}} = \text{Marketing \% of CAC}$$

Now, use the same figures as in the last example, but assume that sales contributed $500,000 to the costs: $450,000 ÷ $950,000 = 47%.

This can be a helpful indicator metric that you watch over time. It can show an excess spending in marketing or sales, reduced performance in marketing or sales, or needs for increased investment in either area.

For B2B companies that typically deal with large sales that can take several months to close and rely on outside sales reps, it is common to see the percentage range from 10-20%. If the company has inside sales teams and a more direct, simple sales process, the percentage can be expected to fall between 20-50%. For online businesses and companies that do not rely on sales functions and individual salespeople, expect to see this figure above 50%.

Marketing Costs Compared to Customer Lifetime Value

Now, review marketing in relation to the Customer Lifetime Value. If your business model involves repeat buying, this is a key figure to understand what return you are truly experiencing from marketing and what you can afford to spend to acquire a new customer.

First, to find Customer Lifetime Value, you must know what the customer pays in a set period, the gross margin of it, and the average cancellation rate.

For example, assume you earn $1,000 per sale, that sales repeat annually, and your average cancellation rate is 15%. The equation would show that you earn $1,000 per year with a gross margin on this of 60%, and an annual cancellation rate of 18%. The Customer Lifetime Value is: ($1,000 − $400) ÷ 18% = $3,333.

The ratio is now simply LTV:CAC. From this example, we can now determine that there is a 7:1 ratio between Lifetime Value and Customer Acquisition Cost (3,333÷475=7.017).

While a high ratio might mean you are experiencing a great return on investment, it is also an indicator that you are not investing adequately in marketing and sales, inhibiting growth.

New Customer Payback Period

This calculation is relevant to businesses that earn revenue on an ongoing basis, such as subscription businesses (SaaS companies, Netflix, and so on). If you earn a single, one-time payment at purchase, you can skip this metric. If you operate on a subscription model, your payback period will depend on average longevity of a customer and the lifetime value. A rule of thumb for cash flow purposes is to keep this within twelve months.

For this calculation, take your monthly revenue and adjust it to accommodate for your margin. Then, divide it by CAC to determine the time period you have to realize your investment in acquiring that customer. The equation is:

$$\frac{\text{Customer Acquisition Cost}}{\text{Gross Monthly Margin}} = \text{Payback Period}$$

Marketing-Originated Revenue

Discovering how much revenue came from marketing efforts specifically, and not through sales, is helpful to evaluate marketing effectiveness. In this regard, we need to know the total new revenue generated, as well as the amount of new revenue originated from marketing. The equation is:

$$\frac{\text{New Revenue from Marketing}}{\text{Total New Revenue}} = \text{Marketing-Originated Revenue Percentage}$$

With the proper technology supporting you, this information can be readily available to you. As you redesign your digital activities, determining this should be a component of your technology and analytics setup.

For a target, your marketing should originate 50% or more of your revenue. This may be different for companies that rely on outside sales teams and handle corporate accounts, of course. Again, this is a metric to track over time as it is all relative to your business and can serve as an indicator of issues or bottlenecks.

Cost Per Repeat Sale

Cost Per Repeat Sale is important for those who have buyers return or for customer-centric marketing. There can be a great deal of revenue produced from existing and past customers.

Measuring the costs of this can help you to realize the return on investment, but I mention it here as an overarching metric because it can transform how you handle marketing and where you dedicate efforts. If you find an increasingly strong return based on the Cost Per Repeat Sale and the revenue generated, the activities that spurred these purchases may become a central component of your business model, as is often the case.

Fundamental Key Performance Indicators (KPIs)

Simple metrics can be used in a quantitative manner, such as conversion rates and leads generated. Attempt to work as close to the sale as possible. However, leads are important to drive to sales teams and accordingly, help us to examine the buyer's journey throughout the stages. Additionally, leads can provide more volume of data than sales and may be an ideal KPI accordingly.

If a bottleneck exists based on a low amount of leads converting, we can identify that. But we need to watch conversion rates over time to determine this. Furthermore, we can determine if lead quality changes by watching the Cost Per Lead and total number of leads generated with these conversion rates. As patterns appear, we can form and test hypothesis accordingly.

> **Guiding Principle:** You need to identify key performance indicators to track at the leadership level. Several examples are in this section. The key is two-fold: take a scientific approach and connect the metric to business value delivered.

3.2.2
Ongoing Employee & Executive Training

If you plan to have internal staff members handling marketing, you should consider having training as a core component of your employees' professional development and your company's marketing investment.

Training is becoming more common through higher education institutions, independent online instructors, and private firms. Coaching and advisory are less standardized, classroom-style instruction and more of a step-by-step walkthrough of how to approach different marketing activities. This is less common, as agencies don't provide these services and consultants and freelancers operate on a different model. There are some firms, however, that offer this form of development as a way to enhance in-house teams, and I anticipate this trend increasing in the market.

If you invest in your team as you should, consider both modular skill-specific training and ongoing advisory. Skill training exists to make sure that your team is apprised of best practices in a subject-matter area. Ongoing coaching and advisory typically begins with an intensive "ramping up" period, then relaxes to regular meetings ranging from weekly to quarterly as a way to ensure your team experiences consistent growth.

Your coach or advisor provides breadth and depth of expertise from an outside perspective who can educate your team while providing guidance to your efforts in a more affordable manner than hiring an executive of equal caliber. Such a hire doesn't make sense for most small-to-midsized companies. Even those with a dedicated Marketing VP may have a specific weak area an advisor can fulfill or provides the added bandwidth to invest in employees when the Marketing VP is spread too thin.

> **Guiding Principle:** Developing internal talent is vital and can have a dramatic impact on revenue. With the prioritization of specialists, professional development and outside advisory can help to ensure you have an evolving team and organization that follows current best practices.

3.2.3
Quarterly Strategy Reviews

What goes unscheduled goes undone. If you allow your digital plans to be implemented and run without scheduled reviews, you miss benefits of accountability, iteration, and outside perspective.

Different aspects of your marketing activities will be reviewed on different timetables: daily, weekly, monthly. However, schedule reviews of your entire strategy are important and should be comprehensive. This includes your leadership team, including the executives across key impact areas of your business outside of marketing, held within a two- to three-hour session.

In these quarterly strategy reviews, analyze the high-level marketing metrics previously explored in this chapter, as well as channel-specific KPIs. Each channel must have an executive briefing prepared, with one page outlining the top three key accomplishments and learnings, the three key elements to be developed over the following quarter, and a highlight of key performance indicators being tracked and assessed.

Discussions span overall marketing performance, channel performance, and digital strategy. This means reviewing all that has been shared in this book, identifying activities that need to be implemented *(haven't yet created a customer experience map?)*, revisited *(time for more customer interviews?)*, or expanded on *(should overall investment increase or department structure change?)*. This healthy ongoing discussion can take place after reviewing the executive briefings.

> **Guiding Principle:** The leadership of your organization must champion this effort for it to be successful and to continue growing and evolving as an organization. Regular discussions and meetings not only keep marketing teams accountable, it holds you, the leadership, accountable to your organization as you ensure it evolves with the consumer markets.

3.2.4
SOPs & Systemization

Standard Operating Procedures become the lifeblood of your marketing activities. Forced documentation of what is done and how it is performed to execute your marketing offers multiple benefits:

- It formalizes plans including what is done outside of one individual's silo
- It provides educational materials and training for future hires
- It enhances your baseline for these operations that you can continue to iterate and improve upon
- It grants you security as you invest in employees who may leave the company one day, so you do not have to start everything over
- It slows people down, providing time for reflection and meaningful thought into what is being done, and this forced focus on quality trumps quantity

With the creation of Standard Operating Procedures comes the ability to improve operations. When confident in their performance, you can then systemize. This is the automation and interconnectedness of different operations. Where possible, automation can help to improve workflows, increase morale, and refocus employees' energies on new and more worthwhile activities.

The interconnectedness of operations is further revealed with SOPs as they show what integrations do and do not exist among activities, personnel, and technologies. From this, you can improve and iterate, with formal documentation of these changes. This activity in slowing down and properly recording what is done is a powerful tool for training, measuring performance, optimizing, and reviewing strategies.

Making SOPs readily available to staff and ensuring they have dedicated time to update the documents each week will help to ensure this is not a one-time activity that is neglected. Each SOP should begin with who the "owner" is, making someone accountable for the updates, as well as when the most recent update is. Then, before starting the SOP, add a one-line descriptor of the purpose of that SOP and how it is related to other activities.

> **Guiding Principle:** Formal documentation of what you do, why you do it, and how it is done is vital to the training and development of in-house teams, as well as providing a process benchmark that can be improved and iterated on long-term.

PHASE 3 CONCLUSION

The guided implementation section was provided to you as a mechanism to ensure you would be ready to finalize, deploy, and manage the strategy long-term. In this, we covered:

Identified the Execution Team:

- In-house and outsourcing
- Restructuring your marketing department
- Budget reallocation

Established Management Protocols:

- Measurement, KPI tracking, and campaign optimizations
- Ongoing employee and executive training
- Quarterly strategy reviews
- SOPs and systemization

In Phase 3, you ensure that there are practical decisions made and systems in place to move forward in implementing your strategy. This is focused on the people involved and the processes implemented.

Actual execution will depend on your strategy. As there are infinite combinations of channels selected, processes and supporting technologies chosen, teams formed, and protocols set in motion, I cannot provide you with specific steps. Furthermore, there needs to be a strategy for how to transition to *this technology*, or how to approach *this channel*, and so on.

However, I can be confident that if you followed this process, you will have the answers of what your organization should do as it evolves in the digital world. In addition, I have provided you with "guiding principles" along the way. You can go back and review these if you would like to solidify a philosophy about each section in your mind.

The missing part of digital isn't more of "what to do and how." It's about "why we do it." Thoughtful approach is the great divide between digital as an expense or an investment.

FINAL THOUGHTS

Today's marketing will be different than tomorrow's. With the rate of change and development technologically and in consumer behavior influenced by technologies taking a stronghold in our day-to-day lives, it's hard to say whether that will ever stop, giving marketing a chance to find a home within certain channels.

But regardless of *where* the marketing takes place, whether digital as it is today or the future's iteration of that, you can rely on guiding philosophies and principles that are timeless. This is what I aimed to capture in the previous pages.

While tied into digital, I believe the concepts shared are applicable across channels. Apply the same way of thinking to traditional media and the principles translate.

Take a scientific approach. Allow for creativity within certain parameters. Be invested in the process, rather than seeking immediate gratification. Do this, and you will surely find successes throughout your years ahead.

Digital is your step forward, but only with a thoughtful approach.

Online Resources

There is a lot of material covered in this book, including some activities that cannot reasonably fit into pages of a book.

Therefore, I've created an online repository of all resources and downloads, which you can find at **DavidJBradley.com/digital-mba-resources/**. You will find resources including:

- A marketing questionnaire
- A sample RACI chart
- A program gap and inventory spreadsheet
- A sample key stakeholders interview guide
- A buyer persona template
- A buyer interview guide

Thank you for reading! When you access the resources, you will also have my email address in order to reach me directly. Should you have any questions, please let me know there.

Best,
David J. Bradley, MBA

About the Author

David Bradley is a unique professional that has breadth and depth of digital marketing expertise with a focus on the process and management protocols that make comprehensive strategies possible and successful. His consulting firm, The Bradley Business Group, Inc., attracts clients ranging from venture-backed startups vying to break into the market successfully to nine-figure organizations seeking to transform how they market themselves today.

His first book, *Getting Digital Marketing Right*, became a bestseller in Marketing & Sales and has received tremendous acclaim among small business owners and marketing practitioners. The book was used on the curricula at higher education institutions such as Concordia College of New York and Pace University's Lubin School of Business. The online course variant of this book has amassed over 11,600 students representing 135 countries. He also serves as an adjunct professor and an advisor to non-profit and for-profit organizations.

David founded Consulting MBA, a coaching company for marketing consultants who strive for and value growth. Typically faced with a debilitating fear of failure and lack of clarity on simply what to do next, CMBA provides the guidance for strategic thinking, effectiveness, and contribution. This allows clients to experience the freedom that attracted them to entrepreneurship in the first place.

Would you like to work with David?

There are two ways you can do that today:

- Work with David's coaching company serving growth-oriented marketing consultants:
  ConsultingMBA.com
- Work with David's digital marketing consulting and advisory firm:
  TheBbg.com

No immediate need to work with David?

Sign up to receive David's Monthly Mini-MBA Memo, a single email each month, compact yet filled with value as David shares business principles, recommended learning materials, and timely updates and opportunities for you. To sign up, visit **DavidJBradley.com/newsletter**.

David J. Bradley, MBA
Managing Director
The Bradley Business Group, Inc.
536 Atwells Avenue, 2nd Floor
Providence RI 02909
clients@TheBbg.com
TheBbg.com
ConsultingMBA.com
DavidJBradley.com

www.ingramcontent.com/pod-product-compliance
Lightning Source LLC
Chambersburg PA
CBHW071030240526
45469CB00006BD/2159